to our brokenness:

may it teach and
love us. may it
never run from
the light we need.
may it never fall
or taste defeat.

–z.k.d

POETRY & PROSE

BY: ZACHRY K. DOUGLAS

through our tragedies, we come out of it as the hero
we never could find to save us. we are the strong
ones and brave souls who wish nothing more than
happiness to tickle our wild hearts and allow us
not to glimpse at recovering completely, but a
rebirth of a mind and spirit. we continue fighting,
because that's all we know. we push forward with
all of our scars and stories in hopes of finding
something that makes sense. the god, bad, and
ugly, all have came into our lives at one time
or another. we are destined to be the bell that
rings to let those around us know that it's okay
if you don't know a goddamn thing other than
pain creates the most beautiful people if you
look close enough to the hands reaching out
to grab a world that seemed to never want to
keep us safe in the first place. but here we are,
warriors of another time, sisters and brothers
of the same struggle. rise with the horizon.
open your wounds and see yourself for who
you are. see yourself for the unstoppable force
we all have come to know you by. it's about time
you own the soul breathing the fire from within.

she has dreams and ambitions that can keep the sky on fire for a thousand years. there is no mistaking what it took to be who she ultimately became, but it is difficult when the world around you contemplates how to stop you from obtaining them. she never dreamt about the day she'd say, i do. she never dreamt about the night where she would stay up and talk to the stars about where to go next. there is love out there, and if you are willing to sacrifice parts of your heart for the betterment of your journey, you will find someone there who will help replenish what you thought would never be returned. what comes next is seeing yourself as the moon does; whole and beautiful. she never dreamt of being alone for this long, but it has taught her how valuable it is to be able to give more love to the soul of who she is. ambitions do not exist without understanding how lonely of a road you are walking. then one day, you look up and see people who once said they cared about you, now at arms length, no longer there when you stumble. she dreams of colors that have the capability of providing the universe around you to become fearless again. she is boldly alive with fight and you will always remember her. love her and always keep to her side of life. a true love story resides in her wings and it is there you will learn how to fly and be kept safe.

i wish you could see me as i see myself. i hide behind this flesh as if it will protect me from these cold nights, when my breath turns to frost and a surrender is heard. i wish you could feel this love i still have for you. maybe it would turn your maybe into, i still see you, too. i am tortured over and over again by the agony of who you were, of who i still feel you to be. my bones can barely stand up straight most days, and on those particular ones, i give my best effort to provide this world all the fucking love i can summon from a prison i have a key to escape from, but choose to see colors through a single window, because in here, i am safe from anyone else trying to hurt me more than i have tried to kill myself. it hasn't been easy being this human i am. a human made to fit into a world i never saw as my home or felt safe to be a part of. when i do care about things too much or more than i should, that is when i hurt myself. when anything less is given, that is when i fuck it up for anyone else brave enough to stand beside me in my light. since the first day, you have always been my moon. the ever consistent pull of the tide and a softly planted kiss of gravity upon my broken wings. i have flown for too long. i have been on fire longer than the sun has been calling out your name. i was once in your life, but now all i am is a dream you seldom see and that breaks me more than anything. but that is life. it breaks everyone eventually. i just hope who or what you break for, still loves you after your pieces become a handful of dust someone picks up along the way and blows on to see how far a lost love can travel when direction is meaningless to us all.

i am a traveler of realms unknown to certain
individuals walking next to me, pretending to
be here. fighting back is what i have done my
entire life and i know with any good challenge,
comes the prospect of being overwhelmed.
i have never lost. i have only learned more
about the soul in me. i have met humans
who have molded me into who i am, and
i am extremely grateful for crossing lifetimes
with them. out of the friendships, love and life
bloomed all over my heart and the songs they
sang live there for me to listen to when the noise
gets too loud. they have a precious way of keeping
it all out. i know my purpose for being alive today.
i plan to live out each desire that calls out to me,
without fear of being judged or ridiculed. i no
longer exist in the shadows where scraps and bones
are given out. i bring light to the center of everything
scared and impacted by doubt, but i am not jesus
christ. i am myself, and that alone speaks to how
long i have fought to be here now. i will continue
breaking rules and remaking them, because limits
are a farce society has slapped us all with. i will
never be fond of labels. continue finding yourself
in all you do. that way, when the day comes where
you feel lost and out of place, you will know it's
okay to keep trying. you deserve more than what
people have tried handing back to you, expecting
for you to settle. love softly. keep your wings pointed
outward. always breathe in before letting go. i was
made by the broken, but my broken is still love.

we are not our past and never will be if we choose
to move with the love around us. there is nothing
worse in life than being told who you are is not
who they want you to be. but you are one of the
courageous ones. you are always putting yourself
behind others whom you help first. the moon
notices each time you do. life teaches us, if we
are kind and thankful for the things and people
in our lives, beautiful dreams will come to fruition.
you are a dreamer i know. it is incredible to have
that at such a young age. i hope you are able to see
the impact you have had on the stars above you and
how they can never get close enough to see what
arresting eyes look like. i want you to look forward
as much as you can, because too many of us live our
lives backwards. you should never be one of those
humans. endless opportunities await a stubborn
heart. being here this whole time, i can tell how
you make oceans swell up with your mercy and
authenticity; creating a new wave each time you
smile. never be the one whose dreams are lost in
the pillows and tucked away each morning after
getting out of bed. be messy with them and
scatter them amongst the wild raging outside
the lines. that is where you will conjure up the
beginning of something madly remarkable.

i remember when we first met and how i would look at you and wonder if fate actually existed and if people actually fell in love as easily as movies and books we watched and saw made it out to be. our lives took off in different directions a few weeks later and we were set to roam alone until the universe ultimately brought us back together. you cannot keep souls who have touched love as one asunder forever. they will always find their way back home again. they will always be able to find the light a heart creates, once a spark becomes wild; by rubbing madness against madness. you are the first person that had ever brought hope into my body, love into my bones, and a future i never could have dreamt of before as a kid. you are my forever flame. a constant source of friendship regardless of the times you call me by my name these days. you are the love of my life, whom without, this world would feel immensely smaller and less meaningful. i remember when we first met and the last time i saw you. it struck me today how fateful both times turned out to be. i wanted to tell you good morning. i wanted to tell you goodnight. i never thought goodbye would find us and our hiding spot. but just like with anything in life and love, grief sleeps with us all if we stay awake long enough getting to know who someone used to be. it is the coldest spot in the bed and the loneliest place in your head.

she is a lover of simple things and can get carried away by the wind if you let her. the way the sun dances in her soul, makes the life around her stand taller as she walks from adventure to adventure, checking for her next one. for this lunar creature, a glass of whiskey and a beach bonfire on a cool summer night will bring the flames to attention and call out to the hearts of those hoping for another dance. continue being the selfless human you are and you will continue kicking down doors that once thought could hold you back. there are lighthouses amongst us all, though i know for certain you are the bravest one. you keep bringing back the lost and guiding them out for another chance at immortality. she is you, and i hope you know how much you have helped me by just being yourself. there is not another person in this world like you. there is not another heart that beats with such conviction as yours. there is not another woman who has your fight and tenacity that could ever compare to your free spirit flying throughout the universe. your footsteps give hope to those in need of a friend who will always walk beside them when the world around them is running away. you are the one people point to and tell stories about how you defeated the devil and all its demons when you were trapped in your own hell. you are a survival guide for the rest of us. only you could steal the moon from the night and have her shine. only you could have more stories to tell than she does.

when the sky opens up, you are the first thing we all feel. there is this joy surrounding your soul that can take the place of the sun and make everyone around you full off your light. you are older than me, but we have this bond and connection that many go without, because humans are too worried about themselves. more times than not, they forget who truly matters in this life. we have never had to complain about it. we have lived it with each other, and for that reason alone, i know who you are and what you continue to mean to my life. the way you attack this unforgiving place, gives me the motivation needed to strive to become the very best version of me. the way you carry yourself leaves me in awe each and every time. especially when the moon moves with you. i am going to miss you when you decide to remove yourself from my life, because something this good doesn't last long enough for soulmates. it never ends well for souls like you and i. not this time. not this space. not this place. maybe somewhere around the corner. maybe in another life where november doesn't know us this well. before you go, just know there is no place in this world you could move to that would make me stop feeling your heart, your love, your warmth for me. our time together has taught me how to approach each obstacle head on and how to love myself more on the days where i feel worthless. the tears i have in my eyes now, are only a representation of the impact you have had on me. where my soul goes, i know i will be in the arms of yours, teasing each other about memories we made while becoming the best of friends, the best of lovers. time may steal certain things from our lives, but your smile, your laugh, the way you gathered courage to hold me, will never surrender their place in my mind.

you were created to show others how life is
supposed to be done. you are a constant force
of strength and undoubtedly the most loving
person i know. there are days i don't know how
you do it all and continue walking through the
flames; orchestrating the fire. there is a way about
you that allows the sun to breathe, as if it never
tires from the rise. as if it doesn't tire from the
continuous motion of being alive. the heart in
you has lived before in a time where souls had
no idea what to do with it, because of how it
went on beating even after the love had left its
cage. you are a woman, mother, and survivor.
i am here to tell you what you have done is
nothing short of walking on water. you are
a collector of pain and won't allow someone
to have it be the reason why they stop trying.
we all get tired at some point, but you, sweet
lady, you have tested the boundaries and
continue breaking the mold of a human.
i will always be here when you need me
and i know your dreams will stay above
the clouds as long as there is a breath
of magic in your lungs. hold your wings
steady without fear. live in the moments
that leave you wanting more. the blood of
a warrior generates the light we are all born
from. that's you. it always has been.

finding your true purpose is the most precious gift
there is on this planet. your words only take you so
far before you come to the realization that everything
else has been emptied in an effort to save you from
killing off any chance you have at finding what it is.
your desire is constructed from the bones of every
fallen star, trying to protect your worth. you are a
walking galaxy and i hope you never live a life for
yourself where you are not happy. we are here for
exactly that. may the love you seek, always know
your truth. may it always know your answer.
with every ache you feel or jolt of life that inflicts
you, we are here to live. we are here to feel every
fucking thing that breathes in us. we are here
to love every fucking thing that comes to us with
a soul defined.by light and adventure. where it
takes us, may we always arrive and remain steadfast
to outlast anything else that tries to take it away.

there is a kind of wild about you that sets the heart
free. it gives the stars their meaning to live on
through the darkness. even if they are dying for love,
they still gleam with your light. where there is hope,
there is a breath waiting to be cherished. before any
human stood next to mountains, your eyes could
tell the story of how they were made. you dance
as if you have always been in love with something
unearthly. something with the power to heal the
broken and save every lost wanderer roaming a
piece of unmarked road upon their journey.
there is you, and all that needs to be known
underneath a talking sun and flying moon.
others look to you for guidance and grace.
the type that never gives up and continues
dancing on the every edge of the world where
lovers meet. there is a fire that lives in your bones
where the sky birthed angels and demons to become
one. you are a miracle amongst mortals who speak of
heavenly things. wherever you go, savor the moments
that bring life to your wings. it is there you will find
a wild one who is finally free.

and when love asks me what i have learned,
i will tell it your name. i will tell it to be kind
to you. i will tell it to never hurt you. i will
tell it to never leave you. there are humans
that we bump into along the way that teach
us certain things about who we are and who
we can be. certain humans who see beauty
and effort in those who feel absolutely
nothing at all. the underlying current
within our lives revolves around someone
seeing you as you are, as in seeing you for
everything you have kept away from others
because you thought judgment would kill
you. and when love asks me who you are,
i will tell it, soft. i will tell it, irreplaceable.
i will tell it, sightly. i will tell it, strong. i will
tell it, adventurous. i will it all the things it
needs to know. i will tell it how you have
always been love. she has been my definition
of it and will forever hold the infinite meaning
of what it means to me. of what it has always
meant to me. i will tell love that she is love.
the most precious, sincere, and honest form
of it. the only fucking kind that matters to me.
the kind that stays. the kind that is goddamn magic.

i can see you wearing nothing but moonlight and
to think, there are other humans who will go their
entire lives without ever truly seeing the moon like
i do. seeing who she has always been. seeing where
her light originated from. seeing where the night
finally found its symbol for love and life. in this
lifetime and the next, it has always been you.
how lucky and fortunate i am. how thankful
and full of gratitude i am. i will try my best not
to overthink this. i will try my best to make sure
you know my intentions. my expectations are
merely us being here for as long as we can and
hopefully finding time to watch and live a life of
our own someday. i only know that you make me
happy. for a soul who has gone without that word
most of his life, i will be smiling when the next day
taps on our window to ask if it can wake us both.
but i will tell it to let you sleep a bit longer while
i find more ways in the light to love you better.

i have found love because of you. i have found myself because of you. i write and write and fucking write in hopes of giving back to you what you have given to me with such an unconditional adoration. my name sounds better. my voice has a pulse. my actions are backed up with more honesty. i've never felt so complete in my life, but it is only the beginning. the only end is created by fear. do not succumb to it. step on its throat and hear it die out with the rest of what doesn't serve you. hear the last gasp of what tried to take away what was always yours. use that breath. use that last bit of air it had to open your lungs and scream out every goddamn thing you have kept back, thinking it would destroy you if you ever said what you truly felt out loud. we are creatures that need release. we are the dark of night without proper light to sing us to sleep. you have become my song, my words, and my never-ending source of infinite belief in who it is i have always knew myself to be.

wherever this journey takes us, i can only hope it
carries us together. we may be beyond saving at this
point, but just as the moon comes back every night,
we shall have our own part of the sky to call home.
life is not fair to lovers who continue longing for
someone who is still beside them. it is not fair to
those who break on the inside long before they
shatter. it is not fair to those who are trying to
help, but get caught up in the chaos and are swept
out to the most desolate part of the sea. maybe all
we will ever be are humans who had souls fall in
love, only to end up saying goodbye to a life we
could have had. the tragedy is that i could have
figured it out sooner before you felt like it wasn't
worth saving. i am here, forever fighting to get you
back. forever rising to kiss the day before your eyes
leave mine for good. where the stars meet, my love
for you will wait. i am too bullheaded to give up
even after i know it is over. it has always been my
curse. it has always been a grave i never actually fit
in. i am too in love with you to ever be in love with
anyone else. and if that is my life, i will make it the
most beautiful fucking life i can, while dying slowly
with your picture beside me. i told you that you
were going to be the last one i ever felt this way
about. i have always been good at lying, but even
i ended up fooling myself at trying to get over you.

you are the most honest thing i have ever met.
you are a human being who is all soul and sees
through to the core of my being. everywhere
i go, i will hold close to me the memory we
painted on the universe's ceiling. it was the
beginning of the rest of my life. it was the
first day my soul was given permission to
breathe again. we are open and able to be
in love like this, because we have removed
all flesh and secrets from the equation.
we are simply bones conformed by the
greatest gift one can find in this world.
i found your reaching hands above my
head when i was at my lowest. you pulled
me out of my own living hell. you gave me
shelter. you gave me hope. you gave me, you.
the opinions of others will never make us change
a single thing about who we are, what we do, and
where we are going. we go as the wild takes us, but
nothing else will ever come close to taking you away
from me. our love united all that was lost for us, and
now, we are only a few breaths away each day from
witnessing magic take place in the form of our hands
holding the only thing we will ever know to be real.
between the scenes of patience, inside jokes, and our
undying love for the adventure we have become
together, our lives will lead us where our hearts guide
all things we have and will create with each other.
every sunset is a reflection of your soul, and i have
never forgotten a single one you have shown and
given to me. a moon never forgets how to love,
and you are no different.

not everything will make sense. that's the beauty
of it. there is so much more to make sense of in
the darkness and chaos, because it is where some
of us have been and maybe still are. i can only
hope you find your way out of it and make
something memorable for the days, months,
and years you have yet to live. may it find
you ready and in love with who it is you see.
may you never be cautious with what sets you
free. we are only here for a little while, so i beg
you, please do not scare easily when it comes
to being who it is others have tried to kill off,
because it wasn't who they needed. we are
incapable at times to listening to ourselves
and our intuition. you need to realize the
angels are behind those movements, those
symbolic sensations you do not always pay
attention to. it's not easy opening the heart
of a soul, but once you do, they will never be
able to rest without the other knowing they
are okay. life gets us all in the end, but it is
you who has given color to the sun and words
for the moon. you are more than what the ocean
could ever be; more depth, love, and personality.
lean into the stars and they will tell you secrets
no one has heard. not everyone can understand
them like you do, like you have. then maybe,
i can understand you, too.

in my time of randomness, humans will ask me what
my smile is about. they will ask me what it is made
from. they will ask me why it is a sacred thing not
shared with everyone. humans will wonder out of
all the times to let a guard down, why smile now.
it is about this woman. a wild and crazy heartbeat
of a woman. i could go on and try to explain to
them why, but some things are better understood
by not needing an explanation. if you smile for
something beautiful, something that's not even
yours, something you know only a few will ever
get to see, you know my smile and it knows you.
it could be in the middle of the day where nothing
is going your way or in the middle of some dream
that catches you sleeping. if you are speaking to me
and my eyes drift away from yours, it's me chasing
her light, her smile.

i'm still learning how to love myself. i'm still searching for adventures and words that are beyond my grasp. i'm still settling into my bones and doing my best to make this place a home. i'm a forever wanderer, with a heart that holds more love these days than the ache it once held. i'm growing older which is something i never thought i would get an opportunity to do. i'm still getting used to the face i see in the mirror and i hope it continues to look back with gratitude and grace. i hope it continues looking back at me with understanding and forgiveness, knowing i abused its memory and its body for too long. i was scared i would never give it what it needed, and if i did, i would end up ruining anything that could ever look at it with love. most days i am still a child who just stumbled to his feet, looking for anyone to hold me. looking for anyone to say it will be okay. looking for any goddamn reason to learn anymore than i already know about love and life itself. you came the closest to me without flinching. you came as close as you could until i took the mask off to look you in the eyes. i will never forget the time they first saw you and how i knew then i would never need to hide who i was to fit into your world, your heart. to be yourself with someone is an intimacy not everyone is lucky enough to be a part of. but you, sweet woman, you gave my demons a home and still loved me for having more than you did. you took on so much of me. more than anyone had before you. you took me into your arms and it was the first time i actually felt mine wrap around someone else in that manner. it was the first time they knew what to do. it was the first time they didn't let go.

life makes more sense when my hands are free to love. they are calloused and hardened by everything they have touched. it hasn't been easy for me. hell, nothing has come at a cheap cost. this life, these breaths, this body, it all has faced death more times than i can count. i don't know how to do anything if i am not trying to survive it. i am still lost to a purpose i believe in, even when it doesn't give back to me. i am learning how to be a man. i am learning how to be a lover for someone some day. i have been alone more than half of my life. i am scared of a lot of things if i am being honest. my own tears retreat back into my face some days because they fear the fall. i am all soul, all the time. i fuck up and have fucked up beyond making sense of why it happened. outcomes to me are nothing more than lessons. whether they are good or bad, they all still feel the same to me at the end of the day. i am in love with someone who cannot love me back. i am in love with someone i will more than likely never be able to say, i love you to. there is a pain in me that doesn't know how to escape, and even if it did, it wouldn't have the slightest fucking clue as to where to go. it just sits inside of me, like a bird waiting on the breeze. i am not a horrible human, but i have done horrendous things to others just to feel normal, just to feel as though i have the power to do something in my life. breaking hearts and ruining humans is something i know, because i have had it done to me for so long, it became my only self-defense. i still hope to love one day. i still hope love, loves me, before it is over.

i will go through life loving you. be it in music, art, or a momentary lapse in sadness. they will all carry you when i cannot. a sunrise means something else when you are watching it, knowing someone else is catching the same colors somewhere else and adding them to their dreams. a sunset means more when you have someone else to name it after. i will go through life finding you in the details, in the fabric of what makes flesh stick to bone, of what makes a universe appear in the eyes across from your own. i am thankful this morning. more so than the previous sundays. more so than the previous breath which held more than a combination of air and exhaustion. i have loved, and to be able to say that and mean it, gives my heart a memory to project on a wall where my art used to hang. my apartment is becoming more of a skeleton these days than a home. moving from here is a beautiful metaphor for what is about to take place in my own life. i am leaving here, but it will always give me a way back to you, back to who we were before i told you i was moving here. going forward without you feels like i am dragging a casket behind me; an anchor of a dead love without a corpse inside of it. i will take these colors, these memories, these emotions from my typewriter, and use them as sails to help me in the miles i still have left to go. i will venture through the next twenty to thirty years loving you as if you are still the love of my life. i will remain firm in my stance, even if it keeps me from a new love. if all i get out of this is a new life, i will have done right by myself for the first time since meeting you. the goosebumps i just got, gives me peace that you still hear me in your own way. a way that you still feel them as i do.

honesty goes out the door with love these days. honestly, i have no other words to say, and if i did, i would use love a million more times and write it down and only use it for every page of a story that is still alive. my back no longer curves around excuses. my smile no longer curves due to a disease i am still learning how to cure. love changes as we grow in age, as we grow into a new age of defined promises and lies. i need to be truthful when i speak in love. i need to be youthful when i speak without a tongue. my eyes cry for something i may never know again. my eyes cry for silver when gold is all i have known. i do not know who i am without love, without its comfort. even in make believe, love knows how to repair my damaged parts without taking away from the original structure. my coffee this morning feels like a sunday. it tastes like winter kissing a sun turning away from its own warmth. it feels like a remedy and sounds like a melody you can fall in love with, long after the chorus has played out. i am jealous of the love i see out here. earlier this morning, i saw a mother walking her dog and had a baby girl in a stroller. the little one got out of it and walked towards her mother, holding and wrapping both arms of her tiny frame around the mother's legs. maybe they have a good life. maybe they don't. but i know love well enough to know there isn't a better feeling than to be loved for no other reason than meaning something greater for and to someone who knows love isn't complete without you. my longing gives me purpose. it completes the end of this page. if i cannot have love, i will be damn sure to do my best to write it and find it in my day. my honesty means being honest about the empty space i still have and knowing why it remains unfilled. my love for myself is present, but it gets incredibly lonely when real life continually shows you time and time again how fucking beautiful it is to share your life with someone who is honest about the love they have for you.

i love you. you have this incredible soul. you are
light, love, and sweet comfort. you are irreplaceable,
unique, and your shine will forever make up the moon's
smile. you are immensely important in ways you cannot
see just yet or imagine, but i fucking see it. one day you
will witness the same brilliance when you are ready to
accept it. i know this because i see you catch glimpses
of it, and it is beautiful to watch. i always wanted
someone who would tell me a story. i was afraid to
go to sleep by myself for years after getting back home.
i was all alone in a nightmare until i met you. you tell
the best stories and settle my soul to rest. i cannot live
without you, but i am trying my fucking hardest. i am
giving my best effort because i know that is what you
would want from me. if i am being honest, it completely
terrifies me. some nights i am staring at walls hoping i can
have them turn into you. most nights i am listening to my
fans spin around and around, hoping your voice becomes
the blades slicing through thick air and heavy breaths.
i remember you sharing a breathing technique with me.
one, two, three, four, hold. four, three, two, one, let go.
i always picture you when i have my hands clenched
around the horrors of being inside my mind more times
than i need to be. you give my hands permission to let go
of the hate they still have for things i have done, for
things i am still coping with. to have you again, to know
you like i once did, to kiss the hands that fought through
what you have and ended up saving me, i would break
the hands on every clock that tried to tell me it was over.
i don't know how to breathe if i am not watching your
chest rise and fall. maybe i am too old to believe in
anything else. at this point in my life, i have no fucking
choice but believing in what a soul feels and sees to
be the only magic existing underneath billions of stars
who see and feel the same things. you are the proof.

love still has your name even if i do not have the strength to say
it anymore. it exists between breaths and heartbeats that keep
my dreams alive. it is everything you are. it is everything you
were. it is everything that will ever mean anything to me. i can
remember when i told you i loved you for the first time and
how nervous and a complete mess i was. i had not uttered those
three words in over five years. i had not allowed anyone inside
of my world to see how much destruction had actually taken
place. i was a murderer of any beauty that wished to stay longer
than i was comfortable with. then you came in and painted and
decorated every wall with colors and feelings only you knew i
needed to see and feel. before you, i had never felt so alone.
before you, i had never felt as misunderstood and out of place
in my entire life. there was something trying to get out and i
had no courage left to remove what needed to be removed.
i remember you telling me that you had me. i remember
believing and truly trusting someone for the first time. i knew
when i woke up, you would be there. it is a feeling i carry with
me today. it is a thought i remind myself of as often as i can.
i know wherever you are and whatever you are doing, you are
saving someone. it is your nature. it is what all moons do for
those whose light has dimmed and become suffocated by their
own sorrows. you are love, because it is how i know you. you
are love, because i still remember what you feel like underneath
me. there is nothing else in this universe that compares to your
touch when you were taking time out of your day to comfort
me in all of my discomfort i had accumulated over the years
before you. you became a symbol of my survival. i have a
few tattoos that resemble your presence and preciousness.
they will never be removed or covered up. they will simply
be remembered for how you helped me take the first step
in this journey to self-recovery. you are the breath of every
living thing. you are the mystic peace that shapes all humans
into souls. without you, my name would be on some random
stone in the middle of a field that no one would care to
venture to. i think often if i cannot remember myself and
all my victories, then no one else will care to do the same.
my ending was changed when you told me, "i love you, more."

she speaks in sunsets and energies only consumed
by distant feelings of remorse and tragedies. she is
a catcher of light, dreams, and all things cosmic.
she has always been a reader and student of every
book in a library designed by heartache and
loneliness. a few times in her life she has been
happy, but the sadness is what she is comfortable
with. the rainy days when clouds set in above her
and birds stay grounded due to the lightning pecking
at their wings. she speaks in broken syllables and
fragmented bones of who she once was before love
got a hold of her. before love became war and something
she was no longer willing to sacrifice for. her hands have
touched flowers with more color then any set of eyes that
have looked at her like it was still the first time. she hardly
ever feels embarrassed by who she is. it has taken a great
loss to become this way. something she is fucking
proud to be and will not allow anyone to feel sorry
for her wings that no longer fly. she walks these days.
most of the time it is to the beach or a coffee shop.
her moonish ways are still enough light for her at the
end of the day. music saved her. friends shaped her.
life cultivated her roots and brought her into motherhood.
though not of child or children, nature is just one of her
babies. the sights and sounds of birds speaking about the
sun to their little ones gives her meaning. leaves wrestling
with a limb to stay a part of a home they have only known,
keeps her mind fresh and ready for the next adventure
should one ever find her. once you lose who you are,
everyone thinks you will remain lost, but not everyone
understands how that is the only way to become your
truest self. not everyone can watch a sunset and imagine
themselves as every single color being taken over the edge
of a retiring day. what comes from that, is the beginning
of every beautiful start to what will be the rest of your life.
she speaks easy and carries the stars with her. she has
become a compass for many who wish to travel by light.

i lean against the moon to be closer to you. i know no other way than to be pressed firmly against you. i know no other way than to become entangled and a part of your shine. i can always tell when i miss you. my eyes swell with immense sadness and my dreams no longer consist of anything angelic or beautiful. i wake up and feel incomplete. i wake up, but still feel weak by the time i roll my body out of bed. with all of these pages i have been writing for you, i am finding the bravery in each piece of thought i filter out of my soul. i have never known anyone like you. i have never met someone whose backbone was made for hiding behind. who would protect you at all costs even if they had nothing left to give to a world that had taken every goddamn thing they had. you became my safety, a saving grace for those who never climbed onto a cross to nail their own hands and feet against wooden beams for others to feel worthy of seeing what sacrifice was thought to look like. you are standing tall, sweet woman. you are standing in front it all, sweet lady. you are standing so i can rest my feet and hands and the rest of me i have used without mercy to travel where i am today. i am learning how to see with fresh eyes that have been cleansed in your oceans. a purity of sorts where clothes are not objects you wear, but pieces of the soul you remove to purify whatever is broken inside. i have cried in front of warriors. i have cried in front of children. i have cried in front of my mother and father. i have cried in front of my two brothers. i have cried behind my hands. you see me unlike any other. you have given me permission to grow in my grief. to surrender the parts of my struggle. to let go of the war that ended up staying over a decade too long. you gave me a life i never thought i could be a part of. each breath you take, is another step in a journey for who i so desperately want to become. somewhere between the moon and unhinged wild is a home for me.

i hope you know that we are made from the same star, from the same feeling, from the same infinity. give me the parts of you that you hate the most. give me your worst fucking thought. give me a nightmare to defeat and kill off. give me anything you want to share with me and i will protect you from anything i can if it brings you the peace you have been without.
you once traced my face and gave me a new sense of grace. you once gave me a new name to say to myself. my two hands have been through walls and faces. through gardens and setbacks. through universes that tried to take me under where death was waiting for simple souls without a bone to sharpen. i am clumsy most of the time. i am an awkward excuse for a smile, but i still give my best effort when someone shows me they can match my humor. i sleep with devils and their angels. i sleep with the dead and the ones tossing around late at night because their demons are all they have to keep them warm. i set my intentions long before i started running away from who i was. i was never out to achieve anything. i just wanted to scream into the abyss so no one would know my aching to leave this place. you heard me though instead. you came running after me as if i was on fire. you came after me like the sun takes on the shadow. you are a true queen without needing extra room to showcase a crown you barely wear. you do not hide who you are. you are amber skies and emerald fires, all whole and set free. your colors are of the helix nebula. you are a suspended state of appearing all mighty and defining. you are not mine anymore, but i can still find you above me when nights do not seem long enough to count all the places you exist at once. your infinity is golden and unmatched. unwavering is your flag, and i take a knee to show you who you will always be to me.

you taught me how love is made when bodies turn into
souls. there are days i know what to do and other days
i can only look out and see what i have yet to uncover.
it is then i feel most alive. it is then my breath feels like
air. you are the first taste of morning dew in my lungs
before the sun kisses it and turns it into your touch.
you are beauty, love, and chaos. everything i need to
remain human. everything i need to keep my wounds
from bleeding. give me love and i will color it with
your eyes. give me a chance to get back what i have
given and i will take the moon by her hand and lead
her light to you. i am nothing more than a traveler of
things i do not know how to use properly. teach me
love. teach me patience. teach me who it is you are,
my darling permanence. i am yours. in whatever
lifetime we have or will have. i am in need of the
soul that calls your body home. you have been a
savior to me. you have been a life never before
painted upon such desolate skies. i was never
ready for someone like you, but the moon taught
me how to love with all my light. we are destined
for something greater. a calling, a purpose, a bond
unlike anything this planet has ever seen. all i need
are your hands when my own become too heavy to
raise a thought. all i need are your lips to kiss me
when my mouth cannot gather enough love for
who it is you believe me to be. i could hold you for
the rest of my life and never need another prayer
or blessing to be wished its way to me. i was born
with a singular purpose, and that is to love you
until a tomb or the waters before me need to be
a home for what remains of me after my body has
given all the love it had been given to share with
you. there are no other humans for me. there is
no other love for me. there is only you and the
moon who can ever call me by my name.

maybe one day, love will know my effort before it knows my defeat. i am still learning who i am. i am still self-conscious about my part in this world. i am still trying on new clothes i bought three weeks ago, because i don't go out enough to wear something different every day. i like it that way. i am made of patterns. i have tattered edges. i have had only good days since being with you. those had been hard to come by the last few years. it felt like my lungs could only breathe when the lights were off. anxiety and depression stole a lot of my joy the last several years. they are motherfuckers. they are a disease i hope no one else is burdened with one day. they are thieves of every fucking joyful thought and feeling you could ever have. dealing with them both on top of other disorders, it would make me think my words were shit. that my emotions were too dark to be seen or felt. that my abilities to perform any simple task would be a death sentence. it's a crazy thing seeing yourself day in and day out, attempting to live your best life when you know deep down, you are bullshitting yourself. i was scared for the first six years after getting out of the Marines. i didn't know who i was or how to live and actually be happy, but slowly and gradually, my life was given the light and assurance it needed. i found my purpose. i found my words. i found myself. i found out none of it was shit. i was merely a soul trying to fit back into its body. never has it fit like it does now. never has love felt as true as when i am able to tell you about how you make me feel. life has come full circle and it has always been a journey back to you.

my darkness will always be welcomed in her light.
she is all moon, all the time. i never worry or fear
if she will see me. i never doubt her abilities to
showcase who she is on nights where the world
becomes a nightmare for those of us who cannot
dream in color. i found you before and i will find
you again. my entirety was made to be with your
completed sunset. you are a vision some of us have
during the quiet aches and wild unsettling moments
of being human. i see you bounce off of oceans and
pull their energies to you. you do not abuse your
powers. you do not disown or turn away anyone
looking for safety or a content sense of being.
you will forever be the love i hope for. you will never
not be the name within these words. you will remain
safe and hidden from anyone looking to find you in
my speech. you have been nothing but golden grace
and emerald intentions. i will never come across
someone like you again, so while i have you in my
life now, i will do all i can to make sure i tell you
all i can the ways you have improved the color in
my eyes. you are not from this world, of which you
already know. not everyone can look at the moon
and have her blush the way you do. not everyone
can look at themselves and honestly love and
respect who they used to be. not everyone can
touch scars and turn them into the most enchanting
stories for others who ask to see them. you are an
undefeated chant, a magical bellow of rise and
conquer for a universe who at times is too weak to
carry the constellations. on those nights, it seeks you
out to shine on. i am in awe of your wonders. i am in
love with you. you are the one everyone calls beautiful
and kind, but not made for settling down in this lifetime.
i shall wait out each breath taken, if it becomes you.

hear me, lover. take my words as swords. take my armor
around my gates. sink beneath your beauty and stay in
love with what you see. flowers rise in your eyes and dirt
becomes a canvas my mighty fingers can paint on to make
you something you can use again when you find it hard to
sleep. there is a bouquet of sunrises for you i have kept
hidden from view. behind my back, i hold the entire
world earth just for you. hear me, lover. take my truth
and wrap yourself with it. lay your head down on the
clouds and rest. you have been in your own head for
years now. there isn't anything up there you need
to remain stuck on and glued to. you are the entire
topography of all the life you have lived. you are no
more a valley than you are mountain. take my words
and use them to keep you from losing anymore tears
over loss. take my silence and wrap your own sadness
in it. though it provides no comfort to me, it will keep
you safe from speaking down to yourself. all things pass.
if mary could find a way to love me, i know all sins can
be forgiven in the eyes of our ageless tenor and spirit.
i am still learning how to hold you, when the moon
will always hold space for me. my arms are useless
objects and taking up empty space if they are not
protecting you or giving you peace. i am lost to this
infinite around you. the one that has me counting
stars more often than years passing before me.
you are a perpetual permanency. all things love and
cosmic. all things above heaven and below its city.
i am all love for you. you could take my heart and
place it in my mind and i would still know where
you belong. i would still know why the hole remains
open. the cavity in my chest only keeps your name.
it only knows your hands can fill it. i am in love with
someone who chooses not to love me back the same.
there is still a quiet pause before my eyes find yours.
it is there i have learned how to love you.

between you and this feeling, neither will i ever lose.
a moon never forgets. a soul never forgets her warmth.
the oceans call your name. the deep blue is where i hide.
i wait for the waves that will take me to you. there aren't
enough flowers to make you the garden of love you
deserve, but i will give you one each day you give to me.
souls come and go. hearts fill and overflow. a universe is
made by a collision of chaos and i am full of everything
around me bursting into light. all things i want to give to
you reside there. today is not only about you, it has always
been your name and who you are to me. there is nothing
more precious than seeing your smile and hearing your
laugh. both are things i cannot go without. today is your
day. a day of everlasting attempts to never let you go
without those being present in your life. love is in the
quiet moments where you catch her reading her book
and you wish you were the pages being touched and
turned. love is everywhere you connect, and i will
never not feel you underneath your full moon,
your full approach, your kiss which made me
human. i thought i was a real man before you.
i thought i was childlike in my own eyes, but you
haven't allowed my spirit to die yet. i knew if i ever
lost you, i would search the rest of my heartbeats
trying to find you in someone else. i have lost years
doing it. i know i have no chance of having you again
like before. i guess the things that keep me trying and
believing in it happening, are the same things that
brought you to me the first time. i wonder often if i
could do it all over again, maybe you will appear out
of the clouds like you once did. some angel's wings
are made from hell itself. all the most courageous
ones escape and bring a kinder flame, a tender fiery
flame, into dark parts of who you are. the light stays
stoic and true long after the feathers leave our bodies.
mine remains fucking ablaze for you.

if there was anything different about her, it was the way she loved me more than my demons could. it was the way she could bring me down and keep me from breathing in the wrong things. i should have been more for you. i should have told you i loved you more than i did. each morning was better because of you and each night left me in a state of mind that nothing else could touch or attack me. i miss those late nights we had. the ones where we would sit there and laugh about our silence. the ones that had everything right about them. i wish i could have one more back to hear your superior smile. i wish i could have one more back to tell you we won't make it in the end and to enjoy what we have now. in bed is where we made our life together. on our phones are where we learned how to shorten the distance between two humans fighting for a fucking chance to survive a love neither one of us searched for. it isn't easy being in love these days. someone always wants more or less of the right thing. no one actually has a goddamn idea of what needs to be done, so we speak to each other as if love is all we have known, good or bad. i wish i could tell you again how i wanted it to be you in the end, instead of rushing an ending that never came. i wish i could hold you one more time to feel your body collapse the soul in mine. the rush you gave me is something i am still after today. it wasn't peace or chaos. it wasn't perfect or impossible. it was the purest fucking thing i have ever felt. i run my hands through the clouds passing through in hopes of it bringing me something that once belonged to you. but all i have are tears on my hands. not from you, but from me.

i would marry your colors and hold the reception in your eyes. i would collect all the greens and blues i could to replicate your aura. i would build castles made of timber and stone on every star that could hold us. your appreciation for detail doesn't go unnoticed in the halls we hang our art in; paintings and frames full of life and who we used to be before love found us. a young reflection of lost artlessness upon delirious hearts yet to cave in. a boundless display of proposal and promise. you are the reason for the moon. you are the arch of every bridge holding more than what we see in place. there are pieces of earth you have yet to travel, but i am hoping we make each visit worthy and undefinable. lonely is something i had been before you showed up with your unwavering acts of friendship and kindness. before you gave me resolute action and a kiss to know you meant every word you had told me. i would marry your feelings. each one a direct musing to my madness and a remembrance of never giving into the temptation of returning back to what i had lost. i am every broken piece of life floating amongst us disguised as a cultural renaissance. disguised as a worn out jesus christ without any thorns to bleed from. i would marry any part of you if it meant having the rest of you forever when you were ready. i would drink the holy water if it meant seeing you clearer. if it meant my demons dying from a death they had coming. i would marry you even if it was to walk beside you and nothing more. never forget that i will always choose to promenade in your light.

like lost souls trying to find love during the end
of a world, we are trying to save anything we can
without getting left behind. nothing here comes
easy. hardly anything arrives on time. i am just
asking you to hold my body when my soul goes
and tries to save what is left of our light. from
the time i could remember, all i knew was you.
the universe created souls in order for humans
to find love. what we have is something death
will never be able to steal or borrow. may the
moon and sun keep bringing us a light to
share for the rest of our days. we will continue
being a pair of hearts, looking for the next
adventure to take us where we are called to
be. once you are where you are meant to be,
your vibe syncs with the cosmos. it is what gives
off the frequency we search for. life is all about
planting and moving forward. we cannot remain
still or stagnate. we have to have faith that it will
work out, because at times, it is the only fucking
thing we have to lean on. when we are older,
we can go back and see the beauty and growth
we have accumulated simply being loving and
kind enough to have given hope in a place
where we were never sure it could ever stretch
out and become something more than a dream
for you and i.

i've had more than enough chances. after everything i have been through, i know this time is where it all comes together. where the circle becomes finished and connected to infinity. we do not always get what we want, but we do always get what we deserve. focus on what is important in your life and grow from there. i am more than what others have told me i wasn't. i am not perfect, but i do try to be honest and fair. making necessary steps to get back on track and finally start a life i will be able to share with someone someday. if you think you are lost, do not worry. we all are. promise me when you find something you love, you will treat it as such, promise me you will give your very fucking best to everything it is and means to you. do not worry or wish it to be something more than it is. at one point in your life, it was exactly what you needed and didn't have. we are all looking for the next best thing, but when it is love you are after, it doesn't get any fucking better than that. i have had it and lost it as many times as the moon flickers at night sending out signals and signs for us all to see and feel. there is magic within us. there is a greater sense of purpose that goes well beyond the bones of who we are and who we show ourselves to be. put your best into love, and love will be your force moving forward.

i am grateful you are here and keeping me company on this journey we are taking. you make me better than anyone ever has. you make my thoughts sleep in peace and halted them from rolling over in graves designed for my demons that somehow escape each time night arrives. to know i can think about you whenever i want, gives me immense joy and love. it fills my body with air and i am off again into a thought about you and how goddamn lovely you are. it makes me wander with wondering dreams of how starry you are and where all angels go during the day when the moon is asleep with our souls. you are my ocean. you are each and every wave that wakes up and kisses this shoreline. i closed my eyes and saw us in the water like we talked about. we were happy together. we were in love. that is all i need when i think of what paradise resembles and how it constructs everything moving forward with hope. that was some time ago though, because now you are with someone else and i am having to maintain the structure and identity of what you left behind. but i will make it. i will be okay. i flew with the birds today, and i found one who spoke of a name i am in search of. my life is forever removed from yours, and now i am walking alone, but with intent and reason. whenever the next season kisses me, i will have found love again, and her name will be the singular reason for my words being about her. she will stay, because when you find your bird in this life, you find your wings. you find a song to sing that raises all the broken.

i came to you with a thousand different faces all looking back at you. i had no idea who i was or what i was doing. all they could agree on, was who you were and that we all needed you in order to be better. my completeness lacks structure to this day, but you have given me my name back. you have placed the pieces back together in a more beautiful way that will always be yours to see and know. it will always be yours to configure how you need them to be on days i cannot find myself. i was where i thought i was supposed to be before you. i thought i had most of life figured out. i thought so much about love, i ultimately ruined it like everything else which had been thought of. you brought me back to center. you brought back my eyes to see a human who never had his own sightless vision. you brought back a heart that had been broken so many fucking times, i ended up putting them on hooks and throwing them out to sea, hoping something would finish me off and enjoy a love i could never personally give. you are a touch of a hand on a barren day, where bodies are simply passing time by pretending to speak to one another. to feel someone is to know you are still alive, still giving life hell, and then the universe sends you someone to heal ageless wounds still haunting who you are. we can only hope for a deep breath, an honest love, and someone to give both to. all of these feelings i am feeling of needing you, bring me back together when i feel a part of me being misplaced by my own mind, my own thoughts, my own disfigured attempt of waging war on my bodily existence.

rivers flow through me. i am completely present
as the water teaches me how to sit with a kind of
beauty that only reflects without judgment. i am
understanding how to view you through these
eyes that have been blinded by stars from a universe
that hides within you. i am nothing more than a
human trying to figure out how a heart and soul
go together. i dream of a love that will lie down and
be still for a lifetime with you. a love that will break
open the sky for you and give way to the moons who
are in love with you. a love that will breathe in a
body and exhale a soul. a love that will look at you
and see where home has always been. a place where
fingertips connect with empty spaces left untouched
for years by those who thought they knew how.
i look at you and see where beauty gets its inspiration
from. i look at you and know why the devil blinked
first and had to die. i see you and know where every
lie told to you lives. you wear them on your lips and
i would love nothing more than to consume them
and rid them from you when i see them tremble
right before my hands find you. i have been running
away for more than half my life. the other half i have
been trying to love who it is i was running away from.
i am doing all i can to make sense of the human i am.
i am here for the pain and magic. for the outrageous
and crazy. for the unexpected and untimely moments
life gives us all if we are willing to go down one more
rabbit hole. i am not after any kind of perfection
from anyone, especially you. i am simply after what
you have held back, afraid of what others may see
or feel once you let go completely of your guilt for
loving yourself more today.

there is this fire in my soul and i am going to let it burn
for everything i love. i am going to let go of the old flame
i had been holding too tightly, hoping i could learn the
way of its burn. hoping i could learn the way of its flicker
and flare. hoping i could one day be able to catch the
light of another who felt and saw mine in the same
way. everything seems to be deadweight these days.
i am carrying around a thousand tombs in my chest
and a thousand more hollowed out corpses who used
to mean love to me. i once made you hallow, a sacred
thing, a precious treasure and creature with a holy
frame. i can barely speak your name these days without
feeling a sensation i have kept hidden and tucked away
so no one would ever know it was you. i am tired of
hiding from it. i am tired of my bending knees and
the religion you kissed me with. i am tired of waking
up starving for you when you only laugh at me and
throw scraps to keep me coming back. i have become
a harlequin, a joke you point at and ask to keep you
company during the lonely hours to humor your
darkness. i am fucking tired of telling myself i am okay
when i know i am not. i am fucking done with handing
you over my heart time and time again and receiving a
few words of encouragement from you. you are happy
now. you are where you have always wanted to be.
in some ways i guess i am, too. but what we had will
never be able to come back to us, no matter how much
i fight for the both of us. i am carrying around your ghost,
because in the end, all i ever wanted was for you to haunt
me. all i ever wanted was for you to be something more
than someone i was too scared to talk to. now your
demons have become mine and i am tired of dragging
them around when i hardly have enough time to fight
off and feed my own.

suffering has always been my choice. i'm learning since i have met you, it no longer needs to mean anything to me. you have made an insufferable man, become a joy in his own life. you have given words to the dead poet who sacrificed more than he had to in order to become a love he could live with. there are days where i think i am enough and ready, then tomorrow comes and i am slapped with a reality where you are not with me. it is a cruel fucking joke made with riddles and the saddest of piano notes known to a musician. each one strikes me in the chest, leaving a bruise as big as the moon that left me at the same time as you did. i know nothing else if it isn't you. i could write a million fucking lines to someone, but your name would be every goddamn word. i became yours before i was ready, even though i told you i loved you first. i was still trying to understand what that meant after being alone for all those years before i met you. i thought you understood the love you had for me, but obviously you were just buying your time until you got what you needed from me and decided i was better off without you. i don't know how to make it back up if i am being honest. i am leaning over a sunset whose colors i am still trying to talk about. i am no closer to being myself when i think of you, when i think of us. i am a breath that sticks out between the fourth and fifth rib, tickling the sides of a soul for a comedic relief to get me through what is bound to be an ending without your love in my life. i have been trying to get over you, but i think sometimes, you just have to let the air out and become flattened by your own desires before you can tolerate someone else's needs.

life is not worthy of being called such a thing if you
cannot find purpose in your misery. it has taught
me everything i have needed to know and feel.
being stuck is a lame excuse for not pushing
through to find your potential. it is thinking you
need to give into what you do not have instead
of being appreciative of what you do. i think it is
fair to say i took a lot of what has been in life for
granted, even though i didn't think i was. looking
back i can see how i went to sleep with someone in
my head and woke up to nothing but more vacancy
for something i have been without my entire life.
i am a pathetic pattern of letting go and holding on.
i am a wretched defeat of life and death that walks
over anything bringing me an abundance of words
i have been in need of. but i cannot carry them
within my own speech. hate for self is too heavy for
me. i am too alone for anyone to find me. i am too
much of a wanderer who ventures off to seek out
magic from magicians who don't believe in their
abilities to bring back the soul they stole from a
human who believed in hide and seek. who believed
in taking a card and writing their name on it to be
found, when it was only slight of hand that brought
it back. i am still trying to come back from the
seventh circle i dropped myself in to see if i could
in fact kill every single demon waging war against
me. my faults are my own. my missteps are mine to
dance through. i do not wish to invite anyone along
with me who cannot handle versions of who i am
that still render me powerless. i am in need of too
much. i am in need of someone who can feel my
love for them without being asked if it is present.

you are a creature who should feel the wind
streaking through their wings. i am more soul
than i am human. i am more broken than i am
love. i am still here learning the parts of myself
i do not know. when night comes and brings
me the stars, i close my eyes and hold onto
the moon, knowing without the darkness,
love would never find its way. peace comes
in many forms, and sometimes, all it consists
of is a deep breath singing a holy hum. hands
hold more pain these days. faces hold more
tears these days. we are not the chaos around
us. we are the light reflected by a silent hallelujah,
exhaled after a war is over. tomorrow will be here
soon, but today still gives us a sweet light we are
familiar with. you are that for me and to me.
you are the break in the clouds right before our
sun touches every single soul looking for a spot
of warmth to stand in. the winter knows us all.
the loneliness kisses our bones just enough for
us to become complacent again. you are the
furthest thing from it. i could call you an endless
amount of tender and precious words, but i know
you too well for that. you wouldn't accept them
even if i found a braveness to enunciate each one.
i rarely speak these days, so i will let the winged
ones tell you how angels even call you what i have
always known you to be true.

when i am done with my life, take me to the mountains and spread what's left of me amongst them. for they know who i am better than anyone else. all i ask of you is to love as if your breath cannot be stolen. we are souls of magic, living in a world that believes in everything but a chance to be ourselves and be happy. there is life outside of these bones and i will find it. i will take my hands and make the sun appear out of whatever storm may find me. i will be here, always hoping humans find love in something as simple as a melody they will sing when all they feel is lost. love is a sensation that never leaves us, regardless of however many times we die because of it. it grows on fingertips, longing to touch and be touched by the moon, by the stars, by a body of water that can call it home. that it can call a shore it never had to miss before. love is golden in a lifetime where color has no name, but a feeling of being needed just as the universe needs a certain kind of emptiness to bring out its full potential. being lost is beautiful. it lives and dances with a dream we do not know how to handle. before i ever saw my own face, i saw yours. i knew then i would never be without who i needed. i knew i would never be on my own even if i never felt you completely and without cause. we are all stumbling around drunk on everything we can consume just to feel normal. just to feel something more than a loss that we will never fully recover from. we are all mirrors looking for a familiar face to find our balance. we are all looking for sobriety within our hearts one last time before we fall again for someone who sits with a feeling and believes it will change who they are.

there's a place my eyes go to when your voice
begins to fade. there are words i need to say,
but never do. sometimes i write them down
to remember. other times i write them down
to forget. when i remember them, the pain
comes back, but my memory seems to love
you more on those days when i cannot forget
how you made me feel when no one else knew
i needed help. there is love for a heart made
from years of neglect and abuse. made from
doubt and destruction. there is a garden inside
of it, where tears run to so they can find their
strength again. we never know how to feel
when pain knows some of us as well as it does.
we never know how to love again until someone
tells us how to live with what has been broken
all these years. it is within these precious
moments, these adolescent pauses, a young
heart strikes a beat again. it is within these
breaths a soul becomes a human. my intensity
is not because i lack self-control. it is because
i am finally comfortable being my true-self.
i can admit my failures, but it will not be
why someone does not choose me. there are
different categories for humans just as there
are with hurricanes. i am not stronger than
anyone else, but my rage, my desire, my longing,
each one can devour someone if the effort is not
matched. i will not apologize anymore should
you decide to move on. i know who i am. i guess
we all can mistake others knowing who they are
after we allow them to sense our calm.

i have been awake since you left. my eyes can't seem to find myself. my hands have been replaced by stones and concrete. my body lays here powerless, unable to get up or think. but i still see you. in this life, in my arms, in my heart, the dream is about you. it has always been about you. i can only hope wherever you ran off to, that you found peace and are without fear. may you be with love and all of its teachings and embraces. being alive is being one with your heartbeat. i hope you are never far away or out of sync with it or your abilities to breathe. we all find what we need when we open our eyes to things they used to close for, knowing they would be there when they opened. i was so fucking scared of losing you, i lost myself before i could even touch you. i knew there was something wrong with me in a selfish way when i could never be close enough to you, but you wanted the same thing. i guess my blindness towards what was actually happening led me down to where i was begging for water from rivers i once used to wash this soul with. even though you are gone, i know my place. i know there is a devil in all of us, but there are few extra angels around me this time around. all i needed was you. all i ever needed was your light to find comfort in what i kept losing sight of. i don't know what else to do these days. i have written books about. i have told the ghosts that follow me around about you. i have told anyone who wanted to listen to me about the poet who fell for the woman he never could hold, so he wrote words to take her place when she was too far gone for even him to locate. that is saying a hell of a lot, considering his love for the moon and how far away she remains and has remained ever since this new love took her place. i will make it back to you someday. whenever this heaviness leaves my chest and i am allowed to move again. i will stay ready, because in this lifetime, miracles happen every day to those who believe in a love greater than what the sun and moon share.

there is still love to be made. there is still love to be
held. there is still love to be found. we are all here
for its madness whether we want to chase after it or
not. our hearts were made to be broken. our hearts
were made to rise again. love is all there is for
humans who make it out of hell before the devil
begins seething and breathing out more deceiving
ways to keep us chained to the inaccuracies it
believes lives within our intentions. this one
time, i walked back to pick up my dreams and
stars i had lost in the nightmare i survived. in the
nightmare that became your absence. i am trying
to find you again. i have turned over earth a
thousand times, but you are nowhere to be
found. i have dug my way to the center of who
i am to find what it is you have done with our
love. life is unforgiving to most of us. it doesn't
know how to treat those who have mistreated
themselves for decades, hoping no one would
be able to use us again the same way we have
abused ourselves. if you have been through
enough pain, you learn to appreciate the silence
a little more than most. we must always remember
that the identity of the heart should never forget its
own face. i now look inside of myself and see an
ocean sleeping. my bones float with peace without
an anchor needed to rest. i remember when the day
would haunt you and you would place your arms
around me, quietly smiling into my chest. i would
hold you as tightly as the sea wraps around the
shoreline on nights where it had been away too
long. i would always tell you, "the moon was named
after you." after the first time, you would never leave
until i told you that secret i had kept long before i
discovered you. it was never meant for anyone but
you. some of us come from ashes, but our fire still
breathes and burns wildly for love.

i am learning who i am around you.
it's difficult when my mind wants to
tell you things that my heart keeps
inside. i can feel distance as much
as anyone can summon a feeling.
i know you are not ready to hear it.
i know i say too much without telling
you anything. i've never not been able
to feel strongly. it's all i fucking know
how to do. when i open my mouth
and emptiness comes out, that's when
i begin to worry. that's when i know i
am the only one out of us who feels
this way. who feels more than the
other cares to admit. i am used to
this feeling though. the corner
knows me well, and i shall return
my face to it and apologize for
thinking it was something else.
in life, i have come to learn that
to cure any type of pain i am feeling,
a fresh sunset is all it takes. it is the
remedy for all of my aches. it is the
home i fall into when mine has been
destroyed for quite some time now.
it is not a replacement for you. it is the
only way i know how to press against
warmth and receive a glowing embrace.

i still see you as someone i will grow old with
one day. some days it scares me how much i
need you. i cannot ask that of you. i could
never do such a thing to someone who is just
as much of a wanderer as i am. maybe one
day we can find middle ground to stand on
without me trying to pull your oceans closer
to my shores. i am infatuated by your energy
and how you can make me feel your breath
from where you are. i am inspired by your
duality of spirit and self. i know i am too
close for your comfort. there are nights i
close my eyes with doubt of them ever
opening again. but i always hope they do.
to not be able to see you in this, would be
me dying twice. you brought a kind of love
into my life that i had never tasted before.
it was pure in every form and held together
my reality in such a way, even those around
me felt complete. we can only hope to find
a love that can see the sun and moon within
us. that they can see the oceans and all their
chaos swirling around our souls. we hope
they are brave enough to jump in and feel
the peace we do when they are next to us.
when we find that, love will be the feeling.
what i have learned in this life, is that not
all the beauty is yours to keep. sometimes,
it goes as the breath goes.

she said she wanted love, needed affection, longed for being next to him. life is nothing more than seeking truth in any form you can find it. life is simply waking up and setting out on a journey inside of your soul and outside of your mind. days turn to numbers with numerical values that never exceed the dichotomy of what and how much you put into each one. she needed a new way. she needed a new plan. she needed more than what was being offered to her by a world not quite ready for her kind. who was not quite ready for the brutal and kindred words being spoken from this woman who never had anything handed to her.
who had everything shaped by chaos. some of which was not of her own doing. life hands out its toughest battles to its strongest warriors. its most delicate faces. its most tangible artists. she was all of it. she had been dropped a few times by others who said they wouldn't. she had been kicked around by her own misfortunes. by her own failures which were not because of a lack of effort. we all come from an emotion, a response, a calling. we all come from a pair of souls, a pair of hearts, a pair of days. she was looking for something to go right instead of everything going against her. a woman like her comes from struggle. she knows late nights better than her friends know her. she knows the darkness better than the moon herself. love visited her only when her face was in a pillow and crying what was left of the day out. she was a gentle reminder to live and breathe. a sudden strike of thunder is all it takes to know lightning is something more than light. it is energy generated from the gods. it is energy consumed by those brave enough to hold on and take its charge. love is no different.
she speaks often about angels. she speaks often of words never told to her. some days, all she wears is a robe, but nothing else is needed when you are comfortable with who you are. it's on those days she loves a little more and love, loves her more. love knows her, because of what she has been through and survived.

cover me up with roses and love. place your hands on mine and tell me stories about where you came from. i am too tired to speak. too tired to feel anything these days. this ache is knocking on every door i have closed. i thought i would know what to do when the sky became blue. i thought i would know what to do when the oceans sang me a sailor's tune. these days i make tombs out of the flowers i once gave to you. i take too many pictures of myself, but i need to so i can remember what i look like. the mirrors can't hold my image anymore. it keeps running down the edges and spilling onto the counters. i don't sleep much anymore. i may get five to six hours at best. i just feel like i am missing opportunities to explore my own thoughts and what could become something special for me. what could become any kind of truth i have failed to understand in the past. it doesn't keep me from doing what i need to do after i get up. i have a new found appreciation for doing the small tasks: driving around for no particular reason but listening to music as loud as it can go. to silence any negative thought riding shotgun with me. i feel like i drink coffee by the gallons now. there isn't enough to give me the mental focus i need when i know what is missing. i find myself all over the bed, all over the couch, all over places i should feel relaxed, but cannot stop moving. i hate sitting still. i hate sitting period. i am not made for pandemics, but i know no one else is either. so i write a million words down, hoping at least a few can make others understand who i am these days. i write paragraphs when others simply hand out sentences to feel good. to appease their attention spans. to garner applause for being smarter than a ten year old. my hands have known failure just as my heart has. it never stops hurting if i am being honest about it. not being enough for someone and them telling you nicely is something i know far too well. at least they had the courage to tell me when i knew it wouldn't work out and believing half of anything is still good enough. i am doing my best at what i was given at an early age. i am still trying to give love.

tell me about yourself. where you grew up. how many
siblings you have. does the moon make you smile and
rejoice in silence that someone like her sees you. where
do you want to be in a few months, because i don't do
years. that's too far down the alley for me. too deep in
the gutter to fetch out. why do you crinkle your face
when you feel awkward. how is it that you got to be
who you are today. i know there are secrets you will
share and ones you will keep. maybe one day you will
feel comfortable around me and give a few of those
away for me to feel comfortable telling you mine.
i'll be honest with you. i'm still trying to get over
someone. i'm still in shameful pieces. i'm still not
who i wanted to be by now, but i am getting there.
what do you do for a living. what is your favorite
part about the morning. i love coffee at first light
and the smell of sun touching the trees. i hate
sleeping in, but i would never leave the bed if you
were in it. i'm scared i'm not enough for anyone.
i'm scared i'm too hurt to ever love again. what is
your fear. what scares you. what is a nightmare you
see that replays every night. i don't care much about
zodiac signs. i don't care about anything if it isn't
heart-lines and highway signs. what is your idea of
love. what is your belief in the stars above. why do
you feel the need to belt out lyrics as loud as you can
when no one else is in the car. it doesn't bother me.
i do the same thing. it makes me feel heard. it makes
the drive less of a chore and more of an event.
it makes me feel like someone would appreciate
these vocals singing alongside them. i joke a lot.
i have a very dark sense of humor. i use sarcasm to
fit in, but it is my greatest strength. why haven't you
left yet. why are you still sitting in the chair across
from me. you smile and i have your answer. you look
at me and i know the reason. they are the same as mine.
where would you like to go for our second date. did i pass
the test. did i do enough to impress you. you laugh and
i know the reason. you smile and i have your answer.

love is everything to me, because you are the soul of it. all of these feelings become fleeting when you are not here. when i saw you, i knew my sky would become different. i knew it would never be the same just as quickly as your kiss completed a story i had been writing by myself. falling for a sunset is a different kind of love. i am all yours when you are ready. i am all yours even after the last piece of earth covers a body that has only ever loved you. i am all yours even after the flame scorches a body that has only ever known yours to be a better home for the parts in me that never understood its own. i spend countless hours researching the stars just to know who you are. i spend endless days writing about you in a way that i hope can make you proud one day. i know love to be kind and promising, but i also know it to be lacking a backbone when the body cannot hold it correctly. you are something holy, something that belongs in a ballroom, leading everyone else. you deserve to be seen, to be heard, to be accounted for. earth wouldn't exist if not for your existence. it stops me in my tracks to see you dance, to see you smile, to see you laugh. i knew when you talked about the moon that you weren't from here. you are the second wind of everything living and gives death a proper goodbye. you are the devil's reason for burning. i no longer believe in heaven or hell. i simply believe in you, and wherever you go, i can only hope whatever is above or below us, lets me go with you. i still remember you as a soul, as someone before the flesh kept us apart. there is love, then there is you. you are the most honest and humbling feeling for any human to experience during their time on this planet.

life hasn't always made sense to me. i thought it was a
fairly easy concept to grasp. love is nothing but chaos
we all try and tame and take hold however we can.
i remember growing up and seeing my mother struggle
with everything that was placed in front of her. over time
though, she got the hang of it, then would let go to see
how far it all would fall. i remember my father would
come home for a weekend every so often and try to fit
all he could within two days of being home. he would
bring presents for us just because he was gone all the
time. i never thought anything of it or him trying to buy
our love. i was just thankful i had parents that did try
and make things work for their children. we never went
without anything we needed, but love was in short supply
after their divorce. when parents split after years of
marriage, you think somehow it is your fault or at least
i did. you never truly lose that blame, or at least i didn't.
i tried drinking it away. i tried taking any drug i could
just to not feel the shame i felt for being raised in a
broken home. one where i tried desperately to put
the roof back on and be both pillar and foundation.
i blocked out a lot of my childhood. some things i have
forgotten completely, but i will never forget what
forgiveness feels like. though i still harbor resentment
and memories from my past, they have led me here.
each one taught me a specific role as to how to go
about using my anger and pain properly. i still have
shitty days, but the god ones come more often now.
my eyes are still childlike in a lot of ways. they, too,
carry scars from before, but it doesn't hurt to look at
myself in the mirror anymore. it doesn't hurt to look
away from love once it is gone. it took me a while to
understand that. it has taken me even longer to know
how much life it takes to actually say you are living,

i remember the nightmares before you showed up. the night
sweats and how unsure i was if i would make it to the moon
again. i had no idea how to cure what was plaguing me. i was
halfway to the other side when you found me. you gave me
my life back, and now, parts of me will wait for your return.
it doesn't seem fair that the universe permitted us to be
together again, only to take away the one who saw me
best. the one who knew me as well as the night understands
our fears. i saw you and realized we had lived before
our moments shared while together with heart in soul.
my broken is your broken. no one has ever warmed me
the way you did. i knew before it was over, before our breath
caught up to our words that you had worn me well. i came
back home half of who i used to be, but it was a certain and
strange feeling how you knew the other part of me that had
gone missing and killed over in the war before i met you.
i feel as though the rest of my life will be nothing more than
getting over you. it was more than love for me. it was more
than a life with you. it was having someone who actually
fucking understood me. someone who saw my scars and
could make love to them in a way no one else could make
love to my entire body. you spent time healing me, but in
a lot of ways, we spent time in healing together. i know it
wasn't easy for you. i know taking on my energy was
something you probably never thought you would have
to do, but i needed you and you knew it. even without
asking, you gave me your heart unwrapped and uncovered
for the beautiful dream it was and still is today. i do not
get to call you, baby, anymore. i do not get to kiss your
sweet hands anymore. i do not get to hold the one
human who held me with nothing more than a glance
at times. someone else has you now. someone else has
your heart, mind, body, and soul. i can still feel you
though. that is how i know parts of me will always wait
for you. through hell or another fifty years of pretending
i am not already there, this ache is infinite. it is spine
bending without the actual break. i am not lost without
you, but the stars have forfeited the night since you left.
my darkness is but a dream, and it is there i see you best.

we go in hopes of finding something greater than
what we were forced to leave behind. where love
still matters and laughter reminds us of better
times. life gets heavy often for me. my chest
tightens and my throat closes just enough for
me to think i am dying, but i am not. it is a
sentence i must repeat to myself daily. i have
to remind myself i am not dying or dead. it is
maddening and outright fucking frustrating
being my age and playing mind games with
myself. it is the act of surviving that makes my
days easier, more tolerable, more meaningful
than just getting up and saying, "i got this."
i need a fight. i need a war. i need a challenge
to bring out who i am supposed to be today.
my body has been dealt punches and been
given wounds many would not have been
able to come back from, but here i still stand.
some days i still have to crawl then mount the
earth on my knees before i catch a breath, a
break, a splendid fragrance of openness. it is
torture, but i have always enjoyed and reveled
in pain. it is something i know better than
anything else. though loss is close to me,
my reward for making it back up is a chance
to find myself smiling again into the abyss
of where nothing grows but everything is
remembered for trying. my advanced empathy
is enough for me to take on who it is in front of
me and who it was standing behind me. life is
making sure you are learning something as you
go about your day. be it about you or someone
or something else, it strengthens the journey.

i miss having someone to walk with. someone to sit
on the steps with while taking in the humanity
around us. i miss you more than i can talk about.
i miss the holding of hands at any given moment
just to show you that i am not only here with you,
but i am yours in this life. i miss the good morning
kiss and the goodnight embrace. i miss how your
face told me i was exactly where i needed to be.
that i was the version of myself i had been hoping
you would meet one day. i miss the sound of the
wind as it played in your hair. you were such a
different energy. the universe had no idea what
to do with you, so it gave you a love you could
give to someone else who felt the same way about
you. there will come a day when i ask the moon to
tell me another story about you. i play songs all the
time to keep you close to me. the same handful of
songs that we found together keeps me upright.
they give my words a new but familiar love so you
are never not in them. i am too far past gone at
this point. i know where you are now is a place
i will never be able to step foot in. you are your
own woman now regardless of who you are in
love with or who is in your life at whatever
capacity. you are a brand new city with lights
that are sparkling with all of the love you generated
since finding this version of yourself. i may not be
able to tell you i love anymore, but i am goddamn
proud of you and everything you have accomplished
to get here. you braved the sacrificing of your old
self and raised a new star in the same sky you fell
from lifetimes ago. i am in awe of your humanly
form, of your textures i will always feel you when
light finds me and hits me just right.

honesty goes out the door with love these days. honestly, i have no other words to say, and if i did, i would use love a million more times and write it down and only use it for every page of a story that is still alive. i'm breathing in a different way. my back no longer curves around excuses. my smile no longer curves due to a disease i am still learning how to cure. love changes as we grow in age, as we grow into a new age of defined promises and lies. i need to be truthful when i speak in love. i need to be youthful when i speak without a tongue. my eyes cry for silver when gold is all i know. i do not know who i am without love, without its comfort. even in make believe, love knows how to repair my damaged parts without taking away from the original structure. my coffee this morning feels like a sunday. it tastes like winter kissing a sun turning away from its own warmth. it feels like a remedy and sounds like a melody you can fall in love with long after the chorus has played out. i am jealous of the love i see out here. earlier this morning, i saw a mother walking her dog and had her baby girl in a stroller. the little one got out of it and walked towards her mother, holding and wrapping both arms of her tiny frame around the mother's leg. she picked up her child and the dog looked up at both of them. it knows it is loved. maybe they have a good life. maybe they don't. but i know love well enough to know there isn't a better feeling than to be loved for no other reason than being something greater to and for someone who knows love isn't complete without you. my longing gives me meaning. it completes the end of this page. if i cannot have love, i will be goddamn sure to write it and find it somewhere in my day. my honesty means being honest about the empty spaces i still have and knowing why they remain unfilled. my love for myself is present, but it gets incredibly lonely when real life consistently shows you time and time again, how beautiful it is to share your life with another soul who sees you when your image is blurred and skewed from staring into the sun for too long, hoping to feel something else besides a cold breeze rushing in from your cracked pieces.

i am a believer in anything that touches my soul and
makes it move. i know a sunset has the power to
change a human. i know a sunrise has the ability to
change a feeling. i know thunder can make you feel
an ocean's responses to loss. i know rain can grow a
new dream within a mind that has gone restless and
torpid. i know hope can reconfigure the heart into
something resembling a fresh breath for someone in
need of new lugs that have gone without a starry
night. i know trust can impact the earth living within
us and allow it room to become a place where we can
dance and run as reckless as we need to. i know life,
its lies, and blind truths. i know how it feels to know
nothing but darkness. i know how it feels to have
your chest sat on by your demons. i know how it
feels to know nothing but hate and resentment.
i have painted many of my walls with their colors.
where i am standing, art is all i know. it's all i see.
it's a new pair of hands helping mine learn how to
wave, hello. you are my new reason to give it all a
chance again. to say hello and kiss your endearing
bones with the magic you have given back to me
by being my human, is what keeps my feet moving
one front of the other. it is the steady hum of
victory i hear in my chest now. a lovely rendition
of a fumbled comeback and an endless source
of meaning every word with a conviction only
the cross you wear can attest to.

i'm a little bit lonely, a little bit too human at times
for anyone to really know who i am. my bones only
show when i am on the road and pulled over on
some forgotten path used by nomads wandering too
close to an abandoned home. my fingers point to the
sky and pick out a destination i will one day get to.
i am the kind of human who misses feelings more
than i do the actual person. i should have kissed you
that night instead of giving you back to the unknown.
i should have held onto my reason for thinking i
loved you a little tighter instead of giving it all at
once. i have never known moderation. i have never
known how it feels not to feel. each person i walk
by, passes onto me an emotional debt they never
knew of before. something entirely suppressed by
time and lack of imagination. something a
childhood could never give to them, but they
found it and uncovered it later in life. they think
they are cursed because they can feel it. i think
they have no goddamn idea how beautiful it is
to have something to remember at all. these days,
my mind goes blank far too often, but i will never
blackout when it comes to who you are to me.
someone before you tried their best to annihilate
me and any chance of me ever loving again.
the thing is, she's never met you and the power
you have. no one will ever be the moon again,
but my god, your light is needed in my universe.
your light is needed in these eyes of mine. tell me
when and i will tell you forever. ask me how long
and i will tell you, until two hearts become a home
for lost souls like you and i.

i can close my eyes and find you in any day of any lifetime. i may not know you through and through, but as far as souls go, i know you well beyond the stars that made you. i have always been a lover first then a human second. i have always been a madman first then common sense second. i may never be as good as i want to be, but i have been given ample attempts at perfecting what was meant to be imperfect. i have held on long after the blood had dried. long after my eyes said goodbye to their song. i have watched my share of movies and know many by heart. i know happiness doesn't always find us in the end. i know togetherness saves itself like a virgin does for the one who truly believes in the same ending. when i love, i am sick in the head, insane, fucking bonkers over the person. i give all i have at the beginning so when it is in the final stages, they can't say i never cared or tried. i remember one time i told this woman who i loved very much, "you only said, i love you, five times when i said it to you over twenty today." i kept count like a lunatic. i should have known then it wouldn't have worked. love shouldn't be a contest of any kind. it wasn't that i was upset she didn't say it back to me. i was upset she never cared as much as i did about something so simple, yet more meaningful than anything else. i think that's where a lot of us fuck it up. we believe they will change. we believe we can make them see or feel love as we do. the truth is, some souls are simply a bridge to a bigger love, a more well rounded version of what we believe love to be for us. i don't feel sorry for anyone who doesn't see love as i do. it only makes the meeting, the be all end all, the final smile you will never not have to fake to get through whatever relationship you may find yourself in. i am not like anyone else. my love will never taste familiar to anyone who has never had to swallow their own blood. when i tell you, i love you, it will have been the fourth time i have said it to anyone and meant it. if i know anything, it is that the universe always brings you who you need right before rock bottom kisses your lips and takes you under. love can try and deny you its truth, but in the end, only the right love can love you back in ways you have been without ever since you welcomed it into your own heart and waited for someone to answer the question resting inside of it.

i think what hurts me the most is that i would have given
you anything, and in the end, it still wouldn't have been
enough. i would have ended up killing myself trying to
make you feel a love you only wanted to feel on days you
felt like it. i remember conversations we had over the
years and each one sounded the same when they ended;
i was here and you were there. i could never get through
one without wanting you more. the connection was there
and it was evident each time our breaths became quieter
as we were getting as close as we could over the phone.
i always kept you as safe as possible. i always gave you
my fucking best, but i honestly couldn't tell if you were.
i knew you were probably still talking to him. i gave you
the benefit of the doubt on several occasions, but who
the fuck was i kidding when we weren't even together.
all i knew was that i loved you. all i knew is that we
would somehow make it work. now i am here alone
writing about how you broke and shattered my goddamn
soul and scattered it across the universe for me to find on
my own. i know you're happy now. i know you are where
you wanted to be twenty years ago. looking back on it,
i should have known you were going to end up with him.
i still remember the first time you spoke his name and
how it made you nervous with him being back in your
life after you had blocked him on every social media
account you had, or so you said. you were scared of
hurting one of us in the end, so you sacrificed me to
make it all work out for you. i will find someone
who doesn't have to choose between another. i will
never forgive you, but i will make sure the next woman
i love gets more of me than you ever did. one day, i will
stop writing about you and leaving the moon in my
words. one day, all i will add at the end and put into
my writing are the x's and o's for her and only her.

when the earth is done with me, take me and bury me on the moon. it is the only real home i have ever known. i am nothing more than a hand with a number within it, bearing fate between my heart and soul. i strike air to rid my guilt, my lack of patience. i have not always done the right thing, but loving you, i know there will never be a bad day or a wrong that could ever be done to take this love away. i have never known life until you took a breath in front of me. i have never known light until your eyes caught mine. i have never been good at anything, but you told me i am good enough, and i finally believed someone for the first time in my life. when i am done with this journey, take me and place me amongst her shadows. i am and have always been too dark for human consumption. i saw you in the sky this afternoon and i have never been more fucking homesick for anything else in my life. you are there, and i, here; too far to love you, but close enough to know you are okay. when it is my time, love will remember a human who found love before it found reason to keep me here any longer than it needed to. my reason is a precious secret kept between lovers. our lives are golden and because of that, our hearts will always fall in love with energies around us that bring out our suns and moons. we are more than the stars ever dreamed we could be when they gave us our light. there is a bundle of magic awaiting hands that remain open to a life well lived by merely existing under what we call cosmic revelations.

i want to live like Hemingway and sail my boat across
the landscape of the unknown. take my typewriter,
paper, and pen and just start fresh; living again.
write my poetry with the sounds of the stars
colliding, while listening to the whales sing of
the waters revival. wishing that time would finally
stop long enough for me to catch back up with the
years i have missed living someone else's dream.
for life itself would be a blank page, waiting for me
to sail away. dropping my anchor only for a brief stay
on some island paradise in a hidden place of earth's
beautiful waterway. seeing is believing they say, so i
am going to go now; not run away, but run towards
this of which i say. if you ever find me, do not tell a
soul. for they will find out my secrets and all my gold.
written in books i leave behind, will be a message:
"to all those who wish to seek, love is alive and well."
we are the adventure if we understand what we carry
inside is the only one of its kind. speak to me in
colors, in musical arrangements, in breaths made out
of constellations. speak to me in waves of blue and
white, in rain i can shed my insecurities and dance
naked in. life is not what it seems and i am not what
you have in mind when it comes to what a human
should look like. i m not after the same things as
you. i am after a chase that feels like a sunrise
birthed by a sunset. we will never know how it truly
feels to live, until we show our souls and bones to
someone who knows how it feels to have had them
both bruised and broken. to be human, we must
embrace the scars that tell our stories of how we
became something more than marks on a singular
universal entity that was birthed with hope, only
to die once we surpassed our time allotted.

i hope one day i can make this a safe place for you. i hope i can make it easier for you to hear yourself and feel your touch, as if you were being held by the moon herself. it is the same way you hold me. it is the same sensation manifested by dreamers, and you are the one who has always been awake, but steady with your ambitions. i look at you and forget everything else i was once taught about life. none of it makes sense if it isn't you standing in front me. i am neither reckless nor contemporary when it comes to you. i hope i can make you feel the sun on days where you are breathing in a darkness i cannot see. i hope your mind quiets for you long enough to hear these words i have ready for you. not everyone will get to know you as i have. to say that is an honor would be an understatement made up by a fool. i am only that when i am flustered by your beauty when you walk into a room only to find me amongst the humanity ceasing to exist properly around you. my hand goes for yours as you take a step. my eyes go for you as you leave the bedroom. my heart goes for you when it skips a beat and you are nowhere to be seen. i know it is you each time it happens. i hope i can make your bones ache less from the constant pressure you put on yourself to live a good life. i hope i can give you something resembling one of those someday. i know right now it is impossible to find any hope at all, but believe in me as i believe in you. trust me as i trust you in every way imaginable. my body is one with your soul. my soul is one with your body. i move, you move. you speak, i listen. i will help you wear whatever pain you have. i am your embrace.

i'm not here to hold you hostage. i'm not here for
some form of ransom, when love is all i am after.
it doesn't make any sense for me not to be in love
with someone who is content with a moon above
her and an open road beyond her glare. time does
a lot of things to us. it makes us foolish, arrogant,
incompetent, hesitant, and kills us in the end.
love does all of the same things, but what time
kills, love can regroup in the breath given by a
single glance. you will know it when it is in your
company. you will see your smile reflected in
someone else's. that presence of life is the most
fucking precious thing there is. i'm here for
whatever is underneath the umbrella you hoist
in the air. all i wish to do, is to turn it into balloons.
maybe then you'd understand how i know you are
worth every single one that is left floating alone
above where we stand today. i do not know how
to be anyone or anything else. i cannot hold back
what has left its cage years ago. this heart has always
known love to be something you actually have to
live for. something you actually have to work for.
something you actually have to believe in for it to
arrive. one day, i will see a smile that remembers
mine and never let go. until then, there is this
woman who laughs as if she knows where the
wild is. she is someone who is rare beyond any
comparison. she is the life of any adventure you
dare to take. she is the light of every soul who was
once lost before they found hers. she's different.
all the way down to her smile, which she hides just
long enough to leave you guessing where you stand
with her.

i have always wanted certain things more than i should.
it is being cursed to love too much or to give someone
more than they are worthy of having. it is thinking you
never have what you need, but knowing somehow you
will figure it out, because you have already spilled your
blood for the moon to see. you have already broken
your bones for the earth to feel. you have already made
a traveler out of your sorrows. my proverbial enemy
has been me and the demons that seem to laugh at the
thought of leaving. i have wanted days to end, because
the night was a better friend when i was lonely. i have
wanted love and all of the pain that rolled in drunk at
3am, when fighting over wrong or right seemed like a
logical excuse not to sleep or a way of showing someone
you cared enough to stay awake until it was settled.
i have wanted a better childhood for the kids i will
never have, because the mere thought of them being
born and mirroring my life scared the complete shit
out of me. certain things i have squandered in the
past come back to me when i least expect them to.
certain memories flood my blood and leave me
stumbling in the hallways of minds i have stayed in.
i once thought i was better off alone until you showed
me how it feels to have the wind touch your skin with
the intention of adoring the cracks it got through to
soothe the humanly ache we all live with. i look at you
and see someone i could never give enough to and will
always want more of when the years change my bodily
form. i am certain about the love you have. i am certain
you will take care of all the things i feel are wrong with
who i am. i am certain i will still look to you when we
are in bed and think to myself how one person can
change the course of a thousand lives by simply being
comfortable knowing there is still love to be made in
the rise and fall of women and men.

i saw you underneath the moon the first night.
i have never been in love before then. i had no
idea what love even was until you took my hand
and placed it on your heart. a shy smile swept
across my face and my other hand turned into
a handful of wishes i did not want to let go of.
each time i felt you breathe, my own lungs took
a chance to do the same thing. it was the wildest
thing; my eyes staring into your fire, lost in all the
ways a human can make another human feel
something as naked as the night without its light.
i knew then love would never feel like this again.
it would never have the new smell, the unopened
texture of a universe mixing with your own.
the thing was, i wasn't scared or nervous. i was
home, and home never felt like another person
to me before. it was always fleeting, leading me on
and then misleading me to where the wrong thing
turned out to be me leaving secrets to keep myself.
i will never know what could have been, and quite
frankly, i am thankful for it ending the way it did.
at least now i know what to do with what's left and
where my hands need to be for the next wish i make
upon a moon that still loves me the same, but in a
different part of the world. i go where she goes.
i learned how not to blame love for not ending up
with you. i learned love still loves after a heart you
kept inside that wasn't yours, leaves for a chest that
never had their own to begin with. to regret a love
means to forget everything it touched. for a soul like
mine, it is impossible, because my soul is too old to
mix feelings and words it doesn't mean.

i not only wanted to walk with you through this life,
i wanted to wake up and see you next to me. i had
pictured it for years and got as close as i could to it
once. every bed i have slept in since, has felt your
absence, just as my body has. you can always tell
when your soul is away from its home. you never
forget what empty feels like. no matter how many
times you toss and turn, some nights the floor
accepts you for who you are more than a bed does.
at least down there you cannot tell the difference.
at the end of the day i am a survivor, a human,
and a man still learning how to strengthen his
bones while carrying mountains that do not belong
on my shoulders. what i do with my life is up to me.
no one will ever understand it, but i write it out the
best way i can. everything i know about love, i have
learned it from you. even if we cannot find a way to
be together now, the room and space left behind has
taught me how many years it takes to develop a new
sound, a new color, a new emotion to project onto
the moon so you never feel alone at any point during
your lonely. my life no longer consists of carrying you
with it anymore, but i still find days where it is the
only thing i can hold. no one may ever get close to
me again. no one may ever dare to tread near me
like you once did. i will understand it, because i
wouldn't want to be followed by your ghost either
if i didn't have to. choices are all we have these
days in a world that takes and fucking takes
without ever giving back what we desire. it is
a cruelty i am accustomed to. it is a life i would
live again if it meant holding you one more time.
our scars brought us together, and they will remain
what connects us until the end.

o my moon, my endless light. how far i have gone without you. o my moon, my forever smile. stay with me, hold me, give me an embrace that can sustain me until we meet again. o my moon, my lasting muse. guide these hands along your edges. guide these eyes beside a beauty they have never seen. you have always been too wild to be humanly loved, but you are the only reason i ever sought after something with the entirety of my soul. o my moon, my indelible mark of madness. you are the permanent use of all my actions. my hands still hold your body when the night takes your silhouette from me. o my moon, my friend of romantic raptures. we have gone too long without a kiss, a tender expression of life with what we have been through. i will take a knee and mary your light. i will stand firm on whatever surface can hold us, as long as i get to hold you. take your time with the love you feel, with the ache you have to pursue more. a universe is only capable of so much. you are not here to fast forward the images being presented to you. you are here to make art from your pain. to live, one must die a few thousand times before it is more about living and less about leaving behind who we are. life and love may never know each other, but the colors they paint for us, gives us promise and truth about the heart that lives and breathes for one more chance to respire in a sunset and sunrise we never thought we would see. one we never thought could care about a hopeful human in search of freedom. o my moon, my countless wander. you are the reason, you are the warrior that protects me from my own darkness.

you will never go without a life full of every sensation you deserve to feel with your mind, body, and spirit. if i get just one more chance to hold your essence, your soul, your beliefs, your energy, your name in my lungs, i will be living my most honest form of life. the ultimate strength of love, comes from someone not giving up who they are, but understanding the other in your life carries more than what they speak about with you. they have been told their whole life they are too much for anyone to ever want to grasp with such rawness and grace. they have been told their eyes are full of magic, but seeing it for themselves has been lost to the emptiness swimming around a wounded heart. if i get just one more day to be next to you, it will be the last time you ever feel alone or made out to be some outcast with no chance of surviving. i am not here to rescue you. i am simply here to get you to believe in the love i have always seen and felt within you. i am not here to save you from yourself. i am simply here to tell you there is nothing to be afraid of, when fear is just love without conviction. we are more than what our human bodies can hold.

there's a place we all wish to get to. a place we all
hope to arrive while we are breathing in thunder
and smoking lightning from the sky. quiet chaos
is simply the soul at rest in-between dreams. that's
where you can find me. that's where you can find
the rest of the wild things knocking on a door
to heaven or breaking in the one leading to hell.
come to me with your broken. let me see how you
feel when the light cannot find you. let me hold
you and tell you about struggle. give me your time
and i will give you another day where love is at the
center of my soul. a universe lays with me and i still
call out to you. before you, before finding this place,
i had learned how unprepared i was for the next
chapter of my journey. i learned i still was clueless
when it came to figuring out how to be a better
human. i will carry more of an urgency than i
have already. losses like that, as a whole, impact
and shape a generation to their core. sadness and
death are reflections of our fears, and i am still
shaken today. but i know i still have immense
progress to make. the power of love is the amount
it takes to believe in it for ourselves. we can go
entire lifetimes without it, but as long as there is
a song in our hearts, we can dance with the moon
anytime we feel alone. she knows all. give love more
breath, more color, more reason to see you when
the sun gives the moon each star, each piece of light.
we are holy in love with an idea of what we think it
could be. listen to the soul which gives you life, and
in return, it will guide you in the pursuit of the gold
that exists somewhere in the heaven and hell we
reside in on a daily basis.

tell them you love them again. and again after that.
it all matters. make sure they know that you do love
them. make sure you know that they love you, too.
say it with soul. speak with conviction. express it in
ways they can feel it. tell them you love them again.
and again after that. it all matters. make sure you
believe it. make sure they believe it, too. say it with
love. speak it with love. express it in ways they can
understand it. tell them you love them. it is the only
thing that matters. i lay my head on the moon and
ask her to tell me a story. she brings her heart to me
each night. it is full of magical emotion. you can feel
the life it has inside of it. you can tell where it has
been. you can tell who it belongs to. you can feel
each scar it is marked with. she tells me she loves
me and i tell her i love her, too. we whom share
similar scars, will always know a story about how
they were all made and where it goes when a feeling
comes over us. a life means nothing if a story about
loss doesn't move you. we each have one to tell,
and i hope you are able to tell yours when love asks
you to. love is the only thing worth this truth, worth
this complicated touch and go of breathing. we are
animals looking for shelter, for arms that never let
go of their promise. maybe we will find it now.
maybe we will find it in the night. there is a great
love to be made once you are able to see the moon
in your heart. where she goes, her light will always
find you. where she is, life will never not know
your name. a love like hers becomes something
more once you see it for yourself.

there was a calm in your eyes and a fire on the horizon swallowing our fears. birds danced on red skies and stars were beginning to show their true colors. we were too young to know what love was or could be, but goddam, we were all love ever wanted itself to become. holding hands with you, i felt human for the first time. you were so close to me that night. before you, no one wanted to share space with me. no one wanted to know why i wrote more than i spoke. you did more for me under the moon than anyone else ever dared to admit. i knew you were able to see my nerves, my attempts to speak without needing my hands to assist me with emotion. you told me to just be myself. you spoke to me like angels do with their own. growing up, i never saw myself in that way, but you granted me life when you said, "you're safe." you were the first voice i didn't have to memorize or run away from. i could always tell who you were and what part of the soul you were coming from before you opened your mouth by the way the wind shifted and lifted my spirit. you were a gentle hallelujah for the wanderer in me. it was then i began writing about you. nothing could ever give me that touch of yours. nothing could ever give me that kiss of yours. we were to young for love, but goddamn, we were the universe that night. there is madness in the blood of a wanderer. it is all they know. chaos feels like love once you have let go one too many times. life is meant to be explored. not witnessed from afar. approach your own heart without secrets. open it to the magic awaiting outside its door. it will thank you by showing you how broken can still be worthy of being loved and loving well beyond what humans think they know it to be.

i now know love's answer. it isn't a step towards you anymore. it is a dance towards what i am setting my life up to be without you. i would have loved you until my bones felt sorrow from the moon's fading light. from the sun's dimming response to her death. i would have given you everything, including my last name if you would have wanted it. i would have went to hell to take the devil out of it just for you. now, love is being away from you. being away from who i was when you told me love would wait for us. we all believe our lies no matter how truthful our lips pretend to be. at the time, love could have been anything, anyone, but it was you. i fucking chose you long before we ever had bad days. long before my heart went out alone that night to break itself in half to save my soul from its pain . you were the undefined, when all i needed was just a human willing to be something more than a reason for love to have a definition. you were everything beautiful after rain. it was breathtaking to watch a sky open up with you next to me. it was insanely sightly naming those colors, that magic, after you. being here, i have found and located my truest form of living. my sincerest form of gratitude. my deepest acknowledgement of self. being here, i exist more than ever before. the ending always seems to cut the deepest, until you realize your wounds are only a guide to protect you from a past that no longer needs to know your name. where you are going is a beginning. where you are heading is a heaven's touch and kiss away from discovering the best parts of who you are and who they could never see you as.

there is love in these bones for you. with the
energy around me, i am still consumed by
the thought of you. there is still a life i
would love to give you, but it wouldn't be
one you could ever come back from. nothing
in life comes without loss, sacrifice, and a
taste of your own blood. you must be willing
to put forth whatever love and loss you have
left, and turn your soul inside out. misplaced
items may decorate who you are, but those
items tell the story of how you came to be
who you are. it will be the most calming song.
the most endearing piece of art anyone will
ever belong to, once they see the material
used to make magic and a dream come true.
there is you. there is only you. without any
piece of your story, this very paper would
render itself useless. it is the only place i
can hold you and love you without anyone
ever knowing who you are. everything we
do from this point moving forward, will
be held on a page dedicated to the woman
you are and have become to me. you are
an undefined shine, a sun flower, a golden
star dancing on a sheet of my wildest
dreams. here you are. here you will remain.
dust to dust. thunder to rain.

i could tell it was like waking up to sunshine when
all you had known was a darkness making love to a
demon with wings. my life never made sense to me.
i was always clueless and made with newness each
day. my eyes sat back and watched my own
destruction. i was shameful and ashamed it took me
away from who i was. i missed love even when i had
it, because i knew something greater, with such an
intensity, was awaiting me. i just had no idea as to
how to get there. then i met you and all of my life
before you, began to made sense. it all fell into place,
like a body fitting its grave. each time we talked,
it took me further and further away from the hell
i was lost in. before you, there was nothing i could
do to change where i was or who i was. people tell
you that you should never change who you are to be
with someone you love. but what they don't know is
that sometimes if you remain stubborn, it will kill
you eventually. if you are set in your ways and
become lost in that shell you live in, all you will ever
know is darkness. i guess some people love spending
their time in places where all they know is a routine
and uneventful memories. i knew when i met you,
i would never be that person again. when you are
alone and lonely, you begin to name your demons.
you learn what they like and don't like. you learn
who they are. you learn where they came from.
by doing all of this, you forget yourself completely
once you are immersed in yourself every single day.
you changed me, and though love left us a long time
ago, i will keep these changes, permanently.

i am not good with remembering names, but i will never forget a face. it has always been fascinating to me, that with everyone i have met and the ones i have yet to meet, i know that their face will never leave my memory. it is a reminder to me that names will take you places, but faces will make you understand life is nothing more than seeing the light of another soul. where we both are trying to make sense of the same struggle that plagues this world. being here has been my greatest dream. i do not believe in religion, but i do believe in finding yourself. i believe you should look up often at the wonders above and around you. i believe in freeing your mind and body from anything that does not serve them. i believe happiness can be a creation you make for yourself regardless of what is happening in your life. i still have a lot of life to search for. i still have a lot to do while i am here. i still have a lot of words, emotions, and feelings to unearth. i have always been good at being by myself. being here in-between the mountains and lost company, is enough for me to forget i am actually by myself. there is magic in finding possibilities where you never saw yourself growing and evolving. i have had many conversations with myself and i am not sure time heals anything if i am being honest. it is all about what you want moving forward with your life. it is all about living in the sadness or finding something else that makes you happy. it is a rather easy concept once you stop and understand it. the pain after having it break you is real. there is no time table and you are not your wounds. do not allow the pain to change you. you will regret it the rest of your life if you do. it took me ten years to value my sacrifices were worth the pain. success to me is maintaining my center each day so those i love can be balanced around me. you are someone i never thought could find me with the chaos surrounding me. i am overtaken by it at times and intimidated by you because of your rawness and celestial shine. i think it is normal to be and feel that way about someone who has your stature and composition.
you will always be the author of my heart.

i am not sure in which direction i should go. i have tried
north, but all of the snowflakes remind me of the times
we used to make snow angels in your backyard. how we
used to make a fire not to warm our bodies, but so that
you could eat smores. my god, you loved those things.
i have even ventured down south, but all the oceans
bring up memories of us kissing on the sand while
holding hands and listening to your favorite band on
the radio. last year i even went west, but the california
coast takes me back to when we were in san diego
talking about marriage and raising kids. this year,
my last hope is to head east to find the peace i need.
i am thinking about myrtle beach. though i have been
there before and walked its beaches, i met this girl
who even had my soul falling in love with her. it was
there i found what love was supposed to be like. it is
where i will go to search for what all of us humans
desire most from our visit here on earth. while many
of us are here searching for the meaning of life, i am
trying to constitute a feeling of love beyond what my
eyes can hold and make sense of. my life has been
given to the wind, to a gentle whispering breeze that
keeps me from returning to what almost killed me
before anything ever made me feel alive. i was
scared to move on. how the hell was i supposed to
live without you, when you were the only person
that my soul had ever talked to. i guess time doesn't
even wait on soulmates these days. to go through life
missing you at every sunrise and sunset, makes me
appreciate everything we ever had even more. but just
know, when the stars say goodnight to the moon, i will
be thinking of you and how i used to kiss you as the sun
kisses the sky every morning. your colors are on full when
purple and blue become a feeling i have been without.

i'm scared i will never see you again. i'm afraid i will never get to tell you, i love you, one more time. i honestly hate trying to sleep without you next to me. for something we had for so long, it went by entirely too fast looking back at it now. a form of love that everyone scours this world in search of, we had it. then we lost it. to have had experienced you, is something only heaven can replicate and i am okay with that. just know my days are made up of thinking about you and only you. i miss when we would wake up and look at each other with those passionate good morning eyes. where we both knew what we wanted was right next to us. it was you and it was me. we became best friends overnight and became lovers in a matter of moments. destiny flirted with us both as we flirted back, because we knew fate had kissed both of our souls. in a life where nothing really makes sense to me anymore, i revert to the memories we compiled in those few chaotic years which will last me a lifetime. i just wanted to thank you for giving me something that will never be taken away from me. even in my darkest of nights, they give me hope that you are somewhere you love and living a life you always wanted, and that makes me happy knowing you might be. no matter what happens between you and i, always remember you were the greatest find of my life. i will forever hold you next to my heart and soul, even if it is just a memory. some people go an entire life without those, while i can always close my eyes and see you next to me. do not sleep on the tiny miracles watching over us tonight. when saying nothing is everything you needed to hear, that to me is the essence of understanding the soul of another human. that is how you allow the silence to lead you to dance as if everyone is watching, yet you two are the only ones who know the lyrics.

i know i may never get to know more about you than i do right now, and in a way, it may be the most beautiful thing about our encounter. the swift, gentle, and ease that comes with words flowing for you. the pain that takes a backseat. i almost forgot i have died a few times before you, before this. i know you have things you need to do before you can give or want to give your heart away again, but i am a patient man. which isn't entirely true in most cases, but to know you are there makes waiting feel like breathing, and i am okay with my lungs filling up with your exhales. you are someone i want to know every little thing about. to the way you wear your hair and why. to the way your eyes blink and stay gone for a minute or two. to the way your hands draw what your soul only sees. to the way your smile lights up the moon and gives her reason to rise again. i want to know where you go when you run from anything you are afraid of, so i can make sure it is safe to return there for you. i want to know what you think of love and if you believe in it anymore. i want to know your favorite color, so i can write about it and give it more of a profound meaning when it comes to life on paper. i want to know where you want to travel to, so i can make arrangements to get you there. but first, i must tell you, i am still covered in ash and smell of fire and hell. i am still washing off dust from a star i got too close to. i am still learning how to walk properly without having to fall to my knees when the light leaves with my feelings. i want to say my heart knows yours to be as scarred as mine, but when all you have held onto is destruction, everything looks the same. i am not looking for another disaster to give to someone who wants mercy. i am still looking for forgiveness to exit my mouth without being sabotaged by my complacency to give up on love entirely. before you, i was a sinking ship, taking on more water to prove to myself i could still swim. now, i am a wave trying to bring it all home.

i would love to go to every city you have ever been, just to feel your feeling again. i would love to see the pictures you took of the buildings and landscape. of the shops and random people that made you feel something about yourself. of the sky and where the moon got lost in you. i would love to see what you thought was the most beautiful part of each trip. of each road you took and the flowers on the roadside you loved to pick. i would love to see where your eyes were during a sunrise on the eve of your last day there. i would wonder if they were closed or opened to the last page of the book i got you to see if you read the final page where i wrote you a poem, telling you how much i loved you and missed you. i would love to know which city gave you your heart back, your smile to your soul, your body back to a dream. i would love to get to know you better. maybe i will meet you in some rundown cafe where the food isn't all that great, but the coffee has a kick to it that brings us a new beginning. where the humans in there all have a story to tell about a girl they know who is like you. i would love to tell them there is no other human like you, but when you have known love, you think everyone is the same. we are all chasing down stories to share with someone who has an entire life to talk about. goddamn, i want it to be you. i would love to tell you how life is still beautiful, regardless of the loss that makes you feel otherwise. i would love to tell you by finding you, i found myself. all of this is out of my control, but if there is a way to write about you, there must be a way to get to you again.

may your life be full of adventure and promise. our lives
are dictated based off of our abilities to translate a soul's
intent on giving a human more than just a beautiful life.
we are alive to give love to every living thing that calls
earth, home. never forget to save some for yourself.
we are at times too hard on our beliefs. when living,
we must first understand the steps we take and do not
take. i am here to learn more and argue less. i am here
to listen to those who are gracious enough to hear my
chaos, then choose to converse with me about it.
expression is the key to life. as long as you feel free
doing what you love, you are on the right path. life is
about choosing to accept what our journey has been
so we can enjoy what will become of it. expansion
leads us to an abundance of knowledge and growth.
some of us are born with too much love to know
what to do with. we are givers, because we think we
are supposed to, when in fact, we are only meant to
give to those who give to us. not everything will make
sense. it's the beauty of it. there is so much more to
make sense of in the darkness and chaos, because it
is where some of us have been, and maybe still are.
i can only hope you find your way out of it and make
something memorable for the days, months, and years
you have yet to live. if i had any advice for you, it
would be that life will become something you love
once you realize what you put out into the universe
is what you will get back in return. do not ever
half-ass anything. life is too precious of a thing to
waste on doubt and ignorance. once you are where
you are meant to be, your vibe syncs with the universe.
it becomes your frequency. karma is nothing but energy
directed or redirected. it carries love in every form.
be kind and it will show you leniency in every way.

a love still breathes inside of me. one made of a dream and an inseparable desire to live freely from soul. i am still at war it seems with each part of me hanging from the noose i tied around each body part to see how long i could go without fear of tightening a need i have always felt. i have been my worst defeat, a body without peace, but still waving a white flag strung together by pieces of bone broken off during friendly fire. the devil still haunts me. my demons still run free. i am captive in my own eyes which hide behind a spine made of broken timber and soliloquies. there is no end in sight, but i am feeling something finally for the first time in quite a while. there is still a love to write about, even if i am without it. it still needs to be colored in. my lines are fragmented at best, but each one has a reason for giving birth to a feeling one may try and neglect because of the weight that comes with being human. empty is something i am cautious of. it a dangerous way to call out your enemies, especially when they are your own escape from hunger.
i am starving for stars, for a universe to shine in front of me. my lack of commonality brings me back to knowing exactly what i am and who i am not. i share nothing with my species other than hands that tremble underneath their own pressure of sticking out, hoping someone comes along and picks me up when my feet become concrete and my knees become stuck to the bottom of a patch of earth that has yet to be claimed. i am insane in the eyes of those who have never felt anything more than a single loss. my absence from my own life never gets in the way of needing to be filled by another human. i am not whole by any means, but i have never tried to place a life where it doesn't belong. i am not trying to rearrange the moon on cloudy nights just so i can see her better. a love like ours goes beyond human consumption. there is only love to give when love is at the center of a heart, caught in the stars. she kissed my cheek last night and i felt the area around my soul heal itself gently with a tender care only she can give me. each night when her light touches these homely lands, it brings back what was once thought to have been dead forever. i can attest to her powers.
it was within my brokenness where she saw hope to love again. and in return, i gave her a kiss on every scar that called her body, home.

she is magic, all of the time. the moon takes
her cues from the soul inside of this woman.
the fight, the strength, the love, the all
mighty cause, all of these keep her from
being just another bird in flight. there are
colors she is still creating. there is still a life
she is after. adventure sleeps in her heart.
a royalty lives within her that only flowers
can see. they bloom just for her. there are
oceans that will never be able to swim within
her. a simple melody can be heard when you
are next to her. one that stars conducted by
shining in a way that lends their light to her.
she talks about happy endings and someone
to love one day. but for now, there is just
enough love for herself and the dreams that
keep her calm and alive for better days. a rare
combination of magic and courage only exist
because it is who she is. her name is
something not everyone will get to know or
say, but she is more than enough for anyone
needing to be saved. we all hope to be like
her one day. she is every beautiful scar with
a story to tell and a life to take back.

love is always going to be the most
important thing to me. i know with
or without it, the journey will give
me a million times more than giving
up because someone broke my heart.
as much as i have been alone over the
years romantically, i am a lover, and
lovers are going to love no matter what.
it is who i am. i am not going to
apologize for not having glass around
my heart. i promise you, if it loves you,
it will likely break in-half if you are in
need of healing the one you have. i do
not know how else to truly love. i do
not know who else to be if i am not
breaking for someone that needs
the love they find in me.

healing for everyone is different. each step more unique than the previous one. if for some reason you should look over at me during a sunset and see my tears fall and my mouth tighten just a bit, just know my heart is trying to remember how it feels to be happy again. any sign of healing begins with opening yourself up to the memory as many times as it takes for it to be only a small part of journey, instead of it being the rest of your life.

i never want to get in the way of
who you are needing from yourself.
my distance will never be because
of silence. it will only be there to
serve and act as the space needed
between two humans who could
not find a way to breathe together.
there is something to be said about
trying, about the gift of time given
to someone who never knew of
it before. even though loss is
inevitable, there is still a grace,
a certain humanly way to live
when two no longer needs to
be defined as one.

there wasn't much she couldn't do. it is why each time she spoke, i was moved to be better at my own life, my own wrongs, my next decision. she could always look at the moon and find a feeling, rather than a destination.
her life was tangible. her scars never hidden from public eye. she wanted others to see what was left from years of battling to keep her truth alive.
she wanted others to know what beauty can still look like after being told to lock away all that made her who she was. at some point in our own lives, we will be told to remain silent, to hide our pain, our wounds.
i hope you fight back. i hope you never need to raise a first or your voice to be felt and heard. may your walk be loud enough to make those who shame you, become proof that anyone who does, will fall at their own last words.

on this day five years ago, a bet was made that changed my life forever and the trajectory of my path. you do not always need to win in order to get what you want. the loss was my greatest victory in all of the years i had been alive. maybe we can make another one down the road. as i have told you before, november will always know us better than any other month or human ever could. it was then, love was found between you and i. it was then, i figured out my life would never be the same after you. looking back at it now, i knew you were different. it was the first time i had ever bet my love on something i couldn't control, and you loved every second of it. it is still my favorite memory of us, because without it, i never would have made it this far in what is now my greatest form of breathing, which is working on ways to say your name differently inside of lines only you can read in-between.

i felt you today.

more so than the days and months previously. i smiled just enough to let it be seen, then went on about my day. sometimes, love is just that and nothing more. which if you have been without it for a while, it moves the soul just enough to where you need it for what follows next. those few seconds of pause and reflection, can change a life. it can save the next love that finds you.

i will write you a vow every day. they will not be promises, but my way of telling you i will never leave. maybe by the end of it, you will say, yes. maybe by the end of it, we can make a promise to keep writing them out together and have a reason behind the days we have gone without the other.

do not mistake her love for something
you believe can be manipulated. you are
either all in or wasting precious minutes
of multiple lives. the hard truth is, when
you misuse someone, you are taking from
countless others; her friends. your friends.
her family. they all listen to the stories and
try and help where they can. the next time
you think you want to be in a relationship
with another who is willing to give you
more than they have before with anyone
else, make sure you are not slowly choking
a heart that needs to breathe freedom.
if you do not hold yourself accountable for
your actions and selfishly push the blame
onto them, you are not only ruining their
life, you are killing your chances of ever
being happy.

and tomorrow she will be back at

it again, trying to pull up the sun.

not everyone gets the same light

from it, but we all have our own

ways of pursuing its brilliance.

nothing more is needed in life

than a love that will make you

happy with who you are.

she has river stones for bones and lilacs for eyes. she is untraveled roads with moons in her skull. she is more than just roses as flesh. it is the way she loves without holding back. when light touches her lips, her truth makes her beautiful. never give up your pursuit of everything that makes you feel alive and loved. some of us may come from ashes, but our fire still breathes and burns wildly. we must wander and remain lost in everything that makes our hearts easy to carry. she is a part of the cosmos, through and through, and before you know it, the universe brings is all back together.

my hands rest above you and then they rest on your
breasts. they have made peace and war. they have
made scars and opened wounds in my life. they have
sacrificed time and felt victory. they have held babies
and the sun. they have dug up bones and buried
friends. they touch you and can feel love again.
they move with you and my body regains its balance.
they graze your fingertips and my life becomes an
extension of another lifetime. they softly find your
smile during the night, and when you open your
windows to see where i have gone, pages will have
been created by simply knowing i get to hold you.
my hands are old with weeds and made of desert
sands, but each time they approach you, they are
unquestionably yours as you reach for them.
they begin descending upon your nature where
there are immense fields of desire and streams
made from the very oceans themselves. we may
fall asleep in different beds throughout the year,
but i awake to my exhausted soul beside me after
searching for you. it tells me the moment you fell
into your dream, and my heart breaks out in
flowers, because i already knew when it happened.
a connection is a string tied to souls long before
they speak or encounter familiarity. it is how i knew
your calming voice from all the screams in my head.

you are going to meet her and she will have all of the things you are looking for in someone you want spend the rest of your life with. she will have days where she only knows sad things, sweatpants, fuzzy socks, and nursing an entire bottle of wine in a room where she is trying to understand how life can be so damn debilitating. she might go for the second bottle which is kept above the pantry, and if she does, open it for her. on those days you will find that you love her even more. not everyone can be comfortable being alive, and she is no different. she makes those days bearable by being herself without making you miserable. her actions do not reflect how she feels about you when it comes down to that. please, just love on her while kissing her hands and rubbing her shoulders if she wants you to. whatever you do, do not leave her completely alone. she doesn't mind being in that situation, but the worst thing you can do is allow her to feel lonely. even if it is nothing more than a few kisses on her forehead and nose, those will relax her enough to let go of the day and try again tomorrow. be prepared though for a long and adventurous evening of being mesmerized by beauty you have never had the pleasure of sitting with. she's her greatest weakness at times and the truest friend you will find. i met her, and she is poetry being spoken by the moon. she is the only way i can sleep at night.

i hope you never have to fall asleep or walk
this place feeling alone while holding the
hand of another who you think loves you.
i hope you never become satisfied with
someone who is lukewarm with their
affection for you. i hope you are able
to understand how loss works when it
comes to losing yourself for the wrong
people. we at times get confused with
what we want and what is truly the best
thing for us, because humans get full
off of leftovers when craving attention.
i hope you are never content with the
view of the water when there is a door
that leads to the waves. take time to
appreciate the things you love. they are
a representation of moments when you
were happy. if you never let them go,
you can always rediscover them if you
are in need of being reminded when
the one you are with is busy looting
streets of abandoned dreams.

XO

i want to praise who you are each day, sweet love. i am sure you have had those stop by and tell you all kinds of things with flowers behind their backs, waiting for the right time to show you how they can kill anything by cutting it above the roots. how they would dedicate so much of their success to you, only to cripple your soul and take out your heart to feast on it. how they kissed every wound, but failed to heal any of them. maybe they saw your scars and thought there were similarities you both could talk about and figure out how it all seemed to match in all the wrong places. not every story needs to be told and not every page needs to be addressed or talked about. some people get it and others are so fucking blind to the meaning of life, they walk with hate in their hands with intent on destroying everything they touch. i am sure you have been told how beautiful you are and how your eyes look like the safest place to be. they forgot to mention the way you gently talk to the broken and defeated. the way you walk after being left to crawl by those who ran away from you without saying a fucking word. the way you took back your right to feel and appreciate the silence more than thinking for too long it was for the weak. the way you look up at the moon to know where you belong and where you came from. the way your smile brings together the corners of a mouth that had been abused by lips only looking for a piece of what you never wanted to give. i want to praise you for not only becoming the woman i see standing in front of me, but also give you credit for surviving all of this time. you cannot imagine what an honor it is for me to touch you and mean it. to kiss you and love the demons that still remain. to hold you and bleed from the shards of life still sticking out. to love you and fight for you and go to war with anyone who brings you pain. i have never judged anyone, because i know my soul is stained and unfit to make any remarks containing a hateful word for someone i know nothing about. but if they ever approach you with a harmful thought, i will snatch everything they hold dearly away from them if they make a pass at you. i am proud of who you are, sweet love. i will give you gardens full of adoration. you have never understood someone until you have closed your eyes and saw their nightmares. it is then you learn what love can be and what love does to those who have to fight in order to make it out alive from what they thought it meant.

i want to breathe in the sun with you on mornings when we are looking at each other, wondering if life gets any better than in the moments we are removed from our bodies. i want to remember how your eyes move when they begin to shake the universe around us. i want to lay naked with you and hold you so i won't forget what warmth and peace feels like. i want to take on the world with you and take off to some random place where we find new meaning and purpose behind who we are. i want to drive you downtown to go on spontaneous dates whenever i feel you need a surprise. i want to take you out to dinner just so that we can share our fries together without you worrying about eating something you don't feel comfortable with. i want to kiss you while holding your hips and bring you closer to fill in all the moments we missed not being together. i want to take my time with us in everything we do, because not everyone falls this hard over someone they never thought could be their entire life. i want to watch the moon sing to you while staring at you the whole time, as if you were the one people talked about when expressing the true beauty of a night's sky. i want you to know why i keep choosing you, and it has nothing to do with your backbone being made from truth or your skin being made from constellations. it has nothing to do with your smile being made from evergreen or your bones being made from celestial art. it has nothing to do with your features being made from wildflowers and rainbows. it has everything to do with me wanting to live with you and die beside you. i want to make sure you are loved the way you should be. i cannot offer you more than that right now, but i promise you, it will never run out on you when you are struggling to love yourself or find a way to open your eyes in the morning when all you want to do is hide your mind in the pillows to keep your face from being seen by a world you are not entirely in love with because of what it has done to you before you met me.

of all my addictions, normalcy was never one of
them. if i am anything, i am a human who feels
everything and doesn't apologize for his emotions,
however immense they are. i crave the lightning
just as much as thunder that follows. i am just
enough earth to hold the oceans inside. i am
just enough horizon to savor the night. i am
just mad enough to keep my heart hungry for
whatever comes next. i will fall in love with your
pain more so than anything else you may offer me.
the type of insanity living within me, is the kind
that will keep breaking me until you are all that
is left of this universe. i will keep finding ways
to be happy regardless of what is not in my life.
the smallest of things fill the biggest holes in
our souls. you incessantly make me feel as if i
can grab all of the stars and plant them in your
heart; creating an entirely new cosmos for us to
explore. there are nights i lie awake and imagine
how you feel against me and how your fingertips
could spark the forest in my chest, burning down
everything i thought was meant to keep me safe.
all of my life i have thought those we meet, offer
us exactly what we are missing in our own worlds.
we can only hope to find ourselves in those
humans. if we do not, then it was a wasted
opportunity to grow. i feel like if i can run fast
enough, one day i will catch up to my heart.

in the midst of life, we discover how often it changes.
we discover how often we rarely notice the good
parts while they are here. we are all out there
somewhere, wandering amongst the reality of life
meeting obsession in its sincerest form. i am my
own way to the world around me. where others see
nothing, i see endless chances and opportunities.
i am odd to what is normal and my heart still seeks
the strangeness stitched by the universe's hands.
be mindful of the habits you practice. be gracious
in the absence of love. be worthy of your own
time and patience. all things happen to either
teach you or inspire you in some shape or form.
always be honest with who you are and how you
feel. there is no shame when it comes to being
vulnerable. some days getting out of bed is my
biggest accomplishment. it is on those days,
i know i can make it. it is on those days, the
heaviness feels like hands reaching for me,
instead of pressing against my chest. it is on
those days, the honesty of how i am feeling
takes me back and shows me how i will
continue to overcome the fears i have of
getting out of bed. being me, means loving
the challenges more than the results. my life
has been nothing more than insanity. i think
if i do something enough it will change. i think
if i am capable of countering my own issues,
somehow they will solve themselves. i write love
letters to a woman who never writes me back.
my madness is not yours, so please, do not sit
there and tell me you know me, when you cannot
read the letters she gets and keeps for a time when
she is ready to read them.

you will go places just to find yourself and realize
it was the greatest experience of your life. you will
learn how to make yourself a priority and how to
keep your boundaries where you need them.
you will feel like this world wasn't meant for you,
and you will be right, because it is draining when
navigating negative energies and people who make
you feel more alone when they are with you. you
will lose friends and family along the way based
on what you believe in and what you want out of
life. they will try and persuade you to become more
like them and less like who you want to be. you will
be a part of new experiences, let-downs, and
everything in-between, while exploring new facets
and areas of this so called reality. you will do these
things because you finally figured out that you are
tired of settling for what you have and make strides
towards what you need. undoing your past means
redoing your present. you can only do it if you are
willing to change for the better and not for
someone who doesn't even know who they
are. be in touch with yourself and know that
the greatest destination in the universe is where
you are in love with anything that makes you feel
happy to be alive. we can only grow if we are
planted in the dreams of which bring us closer
to the light.

.inhale.exhale.move.

i wonder how long your eyes have looked for mine without ever knowing my name. i wonder what it must have been like for you to walk all this way without learning of my existence prior to your voyage. i wonder how exhausting it was to climb over the lies and fall flat on your back into a pile of thrown away yesterdays. i wonder how long i can hold your hand until it becomes a part of me. even after all of my wondering, i will still be in awe of the woman you are and what you have been through to smile the way you do. love may not be present in your life today, but if hell let go of my throat, there is still hope for you to find whatever it is you are after. anything is possible when life itself falls for a soul and not an outcome. we are where the universe starts, and we will be where it ends. until then, go after the sparks of the night. it is there where you will feel me if you ever feel alone.

sweet soul,

adventures were made to be chased, not wished for. experience the wind while you can still fly. while you still have neon in your veins. while you still have stories dying to speak your name. you are made from the dust, tress, water, flowers, and all things free. believe you are, and you will see how the sky is only there as a reminder to live the hell out of whatever life you want. do not die with wild still left in your butterfly bones.

i will run my hands over you until your body
becomes them and cannot hold anything else
but our love. i will continue to look at you and
see a goddess who lives inside of your insecurities.
my lips will remain pressed against your own until
the air we breathe becomes the death of our words.
i would love to lie naked with you in bed for days
on end to be able to experience every sensation we
can generate by being the version of who we are
now. your skin smells of magic. your heartbeat
sounds like mother earth. your whispers feel like
the night dancing on the moon. your body
intertwined with mine is how a soul escapes the
torture of being locked inside of skin they never
wanted to be in at the beginning. come with me,
sweet woman, and we will raise the stars together.
we will venture out underneath the sky to find
who it is we must become to keep them alive.
lost love still lingers amongst the angels and
devils living within us. i am at my beat when
love becomes each breath i exhale with you.
we are not here to be remembered. we are
here to learn how to live for the now. we are
still shedding demons that have tried to pull
us under. we are still in a stage of grief, but
today, we are the flowers, instead of what they
once tried to put into a casket. this morning,
i gave thanks to the universe and the way our
stars gracefully keep their playfulness.

whatever they told you. whatever they
did to you that made you break and fall
beyond the edges of the universe, you
deserve the healing. you deserve someone
who will continue to help you back up,
time and time again, just to show you
how it feels to never second guess your
love or actions. you deserve someone
who you can talk about what hurts and
aches inside of you without them thinking
you are weak and fragile for being human.
you deserve someone who can be your
backbone when you feel like bending
in-half to avoid what is out there.
you deserve someone whose hands will
never raise, and if they do, it is to only
lift you above the stars where you belong.
you deserve someone whose voice doesn't
make you cower in fear because what you
said didn't please them. you deserve healing,
and beyond that, you deserve to be loved
for being yourself. you will find this, and
when you do, fall as hard as you can into
a life you had been deprived of, a freedom
you were denounced from, and a love you
were born for.

maybe you won't ever understand her or why she does
the things that set her free, but this world was birthed
by chaos with intentions of giving this true wanderer a
heart everyone can see. she sleeps naked most nights
just to feel the pureness of the light. sometimes she
simply wants to feel nothing, but knows how toxic it
can be to keep your demons chained to the backbone
of your dreams. she's curious about the structure of
love and how one gives so much without it ever being
returned. there's this innocence in her touch that
makes you believe she's never been held properly
when loneliness became sounds of thunder. she's most
comfortable when nothing goes as planned and still has
no regrets when it comes to how she burns for what she
loves. as long as her feet are touching the shore of some
distant adventure, everything is exactly how it should be.
she travels to stay lost, because there's no such thing as
being found when it comes to living and laughing your
way to who you need to be. she's not ready to settle
down or settle at all. when you already have everything,
you learn how to make do without the lies others are
born to tell. she's the source of every beginning and
where all things go to learn about a woman who scaled
mountains and swam in oceans others wish for during
the months of boredom. being herself has been her
greatest discovery. one of which came with immense
suffering, though her smile tells a different story.
there are still changes to make, but those are for
the people she lets in, the ones only she can keep.

i get nervous i am not outgoing enough for you and that it may interfere with things we will want to do one day. i am not always this way, but i allow my mind to formulate negativity and cultivate doubt in abundance for a reason i cannot tell you other than i am my own worst enemy. i never thought i would have been able to do the things i have done since meeting you. i will be five years sober this october. i will have been clean from cigarettes for close to six years. i have written several books and in the infant stages of breathing again. i still find myself being anxious about certain things, even though we connect on a deeper level than the three feet of water i had been used to in the past. i crave this type of vibe we share and to have it at my age now, i know i will never settle for anything other than this. our personalities are polar opposites of one another, but we enjoy a similar life. i can be a troubled human, but i am solely yours in a world that understands nothing more than taking the easy way, because anything else isn't worth the time to make it last. i oftentimes become paralyzed and transfixed on thoughts of us and how we can make it work while not being together in this present moment. i have been known to second guess myself. it started at an early age when i thought i was one of the reasons my parents split up. i am me, and i know you have said a million times that is enough for you, but i just have a hard time believing what you see when you look at me and i look at you. women of your stature and beauty don't exist in my universe. when you walked into it, you created a whole new reason to love my life, even after i came back from walking with the dead. you deserve more than i can offer at this point or any other, but you still remain planted here. i am here because you exist, and i can only hope you will always see my heart and soul every time you are beside me. am i scared? fuck yes i am. but you have this gentleness about you which makes the unusual and monstrous parts of who i am seem impeccably arranged for your life. i may get unnerved from time to time, but it is only because you are above my total comprehension of reality. though sometimes, unthinkable things happen to those who have only experienced love through pain and heartache. sometimes, the universe sends you someone to break open the bottle which had enclosed your message and purpose for still being here.

even under the moon, stories are told about how life is made to be lived. if you walk far enough, you may run into yourself one day. images of who we are can be found painted on any surface. it is what leads us on these adventures of freedom. these excursions demand our patience, our truths, our unparalleled yearning for discovery. if you run into me, it means i have already found what you are looking for.
we are all still after something even after the initial unearthing. fall in love with anything that moves your soul to where it can be seen, felt, and heard. i didn't know how much hell i would have to go through to be where i am at now. i took the devil's horns as a souvenir and reminder that life is only fair to those who never live. even when all that is left of the day is a single star welcoming in the moon, i will look to the horizon of my life and open my eyes to take you in. i will hold you again. one star will always be enough for me to know just how lucky i am to be alive and thankful for you tonight. to be grateful you didn't give up your search when you thought about walking back to where you came from, instead of moving forward with the wind that kept you alive. there will be days your mind will replace your heart and make you feel things that do not exist. we are souls first. you mustn't forget what is inside, gives life to the outside. what we see, reflects more than flesh. it gives purpose to the details we at times pay no attention to. believe in your truth and dance wildly for it all. strangers is a loose term when it comes to souls. we all know each other in some way, shape, or form.

nothing feels better than knowing you are living your best life. give yourself the love, commitment, and relationship that will provide you with it all. if you find yourself being the best option for those things at this time, live it beautifully and regret free. sometimes, we are who we need when everything you feel, feels like a dead end road. once you locate the beginning, the finality ceases to scare away the possibilities you may never discover if you continue to fear the loneliness as meaning being without someone else. being absent from your own life is an open invitation for others to leave you the just the same. at the end of the day, we are all trying to get over someone. oftentimes, it is who you could have been. our lives are shaped by the loss, but it typically creates a fire even our sun cannot withstand. grow inward, then you can expand your own life outwardly as far as your soul can dream. only we can give meaning to our struggles and victories. what a fucking gift it is to have perception when dealing in pain. go through life avoiding giving the same ache to those who only wish to give you love. it is a better way of breathing for everyone if we learn how much our lungs can carry before they collapse before our bodies are ready to give up. you are not your darkest days. the sun lives in us all, even when you feel you are without its light. every horizon catches the rays differently, just as our hearts captures colors only a dying day can give us. our love will always matter, regardless if it is for self, reason, human, or dream. it calls on us to give all we have so something else can be inspired to keep living.

anxiety kisses me and my nerves hug the last ounce of strength my hungry bones carry. i move in and out of the world like bubbles being blown from little kids learning love and appreciation for the smaller things in life. i have room to run, but a sunset can never be caught if you do not understand the power behind it. i hold onto a dream i had when I was twelve. i hold onto a childhood divorce that wasn't my fault. i hold onto a family that never knew how to be there as a whole. i am now who i needed when i was hurting and crying into a pillow that valued my tears and never asked a question until i was done. depression asked me how i was today and i smiled without giving it anymore thought. my mind is a parade of colors and symbols dancing by themselves, because they are afraid to ask the other to the floor. certain music plays, and i am home. certain fragrances attach themselves to my senses, and i am home. certain words taste like maturity, and i am home. i no longer feel like my childhood. sometimes, that is a good thing, but some days you need to feel the past to protect you from a future not suited for your eyes. when i forgot how to pronounce the name of my spirit, i found escape in your presence. i found a gathering of such profound comfort, i dropped the fear to embrace your body. now, we are closer than stars touching water. you will always be beyond a miracle for lost travelers of cursed hearts who finally gain steady courage to rest and regroup.

may your love be the kind that guides and never
distracts from the journey someone is on. may you
find yourself with earth in your eyes, flowers in your
hands, and a reason to begin a better life. may the
day kiss your lips with such an adoration, that you
forget how it feels to hurt. wherever this life takes
you, i hope you find a place where you can finally
fit in. being human means breathing even when
your lungs are afraid to. find a way to be happy
and love yourself. we are all deserving of someone
beautiful and unforgettable. we all need our own
magic when the day gives us its last piece of it.
when you grow, i grow. we are a garden of wild,
where love waters the soul. i am not here to keep
you from the sun. you are all of the light in my sky.
i am still unsure of what i am doing, but my failure
is nothing more than learning how to love myself
after it. i will keep walking without fear. my purpose
is love, and as long as it breathes in me, i will breathe
for you. being grounded is what keeps the earth in us
free. life is nothing more than continually running
into yourself and finding new ways to love who you
see. to live, you have to love and feel. it is why we are
created. it's not always easy, and more times than not,
the hurt will overwhelm you. we are here to risk it all;
soul, bones, and heart. we are here to have that one
chance of being honestly accepted for the human we
are. the only thing i am sure of at this point, is this
heart living inside of me, beats for adventure without
skipping over details which makes this life worthy of
exploring. anything else, i am failing as a human.

i want to take more road trips and fall in love with more
sunsets. i want to get lost in the city and walk for hours
while never finding my way back to where i started. i want
to see new things and new faces who don't know my name.
i want a fresh start where the sun still remembers me, but
the past is kept at bay. i want to sleep under the stars with
a fire telling me stories of how the earth gives to those who
give back to it. i want to talk to people who do not view the
world as i do and understand them better and not be like
those who hate because that is all they know. i want to take
a balloon to the moon and meet you there to show you the
power of imagination and how it can create the most
memorable experiences of your life. i want to be less gullible
and actually live for myself. i want to take care of my bones,
but if they should ever break, i hope it is for the adventure
of my life. i want to know why we run away from it all when
running is what brought us here in the first place. i want to
take my clothes off and swim with you in the ocean and hold
you while the waves chase after us for once. i want to learn
new languages and eat more junk food. i want more
randomness than planning a lifetime that may or may not
work out. i want to be able to speak of a life i fought for
rather than one that was given to me. i want to fail and be
proud of the effort i made to do something out of my
comfort zone. i want to see you day in and day out for
the rest of my breaths. i want more than i need, and i
do not know if that is a bad thing or not. the heart can
be misunderstood when you are faking a life you think
you are a part of, just to be happily accessible to people
who may or may not care for you. i want people to wear
whatever they want to my funeral when that day comes.
i want to be early to everything so i never have the chance
of missing out on the pureness of love. i want to wake up
and see you there with me dreaming of every goddamn
magical thing our starving souls can conjure up. i want
to explore your body and then the world. none of it is
worth a damn if you are not ready for the setbacks.
i want it all.

she tells me wine solves everything. whether it is a glass right before noon or 2am, it puts things back in order. give her a few hours to decompress when she gets home and allow her to change into her fuzzy socks and bathrobe. allow her heart to settle and the wine to breathe before confronting her about anything that can wait. tell her you love her and let her be. if she needs you, she won't have to ask you. give her time with at least a few glasses before approaching her. she's not trying to be sexy for you when her day damn near took all of her energy and sanity. she's not trying to be short with you when she gets into her pajamas and doesn't give you a chance to say anything. humans have a funny way of fucking up what you thought was going to be a perfect day. give her time to herself and she will repay you tenfold. she won't always have those days. she won't always want to drink the entire bottle just to put her tears inside and say goodnight to everything. sometimes, she will have a glass and kiss the day off of you. sometimes, she will have two glasses and take advantage of you, because she knows you cannot resist any side of her. sometimes, she will have three glasses, read half of her book, write down some things in her journal, and will be waiting for you to snuggle with her. life won't always give you those days and it's nothing you did. she is a rare breed who devours what she loves when the time calls for it. the crazy part is, you won't know how to engage with each one of those situations, but she will give you signs as to how to handle each one of them. a woman like her has all kinds of layers you are unaware of until she wants you to know why. she is a combination of stardust and sin, a wishful dreamer who gets what she wants, when she wants it. it has nothing to do with her being vain or conceited. self-respect always looks different to those who have none for themselves. being judged doesn't keep her up at night. it's all about the promise to awake the next day, with a fire brighter than the day before which tried to kill her. it will never be able to match her flames. some fires you must sit with and be patient towards if you ever want to truly feel the warmth it is meant to give off.

before our bodies caged the essence of who we were, sincerity kissed our souls and promised we would always be together. before we lost each other, the world was in the infant stages of a beginning we weren't sure we wanted to be a part of. confusion kicked us in the guts before we had a chance to say goodbye. i still have the imprint of the ache it left behind. it was the place where you used to lay your head and sleep while i played with your hair and watched the shadows leave us. love used to cry out through our voices before silence adopted a new reality for you and i. we were torn from a promise we made and now the search is on again to find a way back to you through the clutter and space in front of me. i have to find a way back to you. i have to tell you again how much of me belongs to you. before the universe disconnected what we had fucking fought to become, we held hands and waited for the moons to rise each night. there is something incredibly powerful about pouring yourself out without fear of being judged. you just know you are safe and nothing or no one will ever get in the way of making you feel like death again. i walk with my hands opened these days, hoping today is the day you walk up to me so i can finally close them around someone who isn't going to let go. we were never strangers, and that's why i will continue down this path until you are all i know and see for the miles left in front of me. you cannot be denied your entire life from the one who heard you long before you had anything to say. truth is, not everyone can sit in silence and picture a lifetime with you. it wasn't just our life we saw. it was everything that made us happy. until these lungs refuse to keep in the breath i continue to fight for, you will always be my reason for the next step.

what a gift it is to find a home in a set of eyes who look
at you and feel the same safety and love never before
given until now. to think of you being without such an
adoration, is to think of the sky without the stars and
how it must feel when the darkness comes for you. if i
ever wish to be known for anything, i want it to be for
the love we both gave to build what we will have for the
first time together. what we will never be without again.
i want it to be with you. i want forever to never forget
the time we created a home made from the brokenness
we kept hidden from others and turned it into something
time cannot destroy. a place where we can finally lay our
bodies down and find comfort in the form of one another.
what a gift you are to be so incredibly precious and kind
to someone whose mind had been a murderer to his own
desires and ambitions. what a gift you are to the world
to be so remarkably loving and giving after everything it
took away from you. if i should be known for anything,
i sincerely hope it is for the miracle you are and the
woman i thankfully get to stand beside. my demons
died the day they heard me speak your name. i am no
ordinary dreamer. my soul dreams. my heart dreams.
my eyes dream. my words dream. my silence dreams.
everything that makes me who i am, has been
dreamt about long before i began filling this journey
with human memories. in you is where all of the light
was born. the stars rest their dreams in the company
of who you have become, knowing they are safe to
be themselves, even when they cannot see their own
glimmering reflection.

i had a dream about you last night. i rolled over to check my phone and there was a message from you. all it said was, "lucky you." i knew what you meant, or at least i thought i did. after telling you everything about me, who i was, and where i am currently at in my life, maybe it meant you thought i was lucky for knowing myself. maybe it was saying i was lucky to know you were out there living your own life. i don't always have lucid dreams or dreams that mean anything at all. maybe it was a reminder to my soul the missing it was going through not having you with me. i know you said you still needed time to figure out your own life. i know you said you needed more time and closure from a past life you had just gotten out of. some days i wonder if i said too much. other days i know i said more than i should have. there are still parts of my life i would love to tell you about someday. maybe we are too scared to admit we care and love them based on someone fucking us over in the past. maybe we roam from human to human, not necessarily looking for a connection, but a stopping point, a rest stop for our tiredness. all i know is, i never want to go places where someone doesn't know who i am and why i am there for them. i am too old for hide and seek. i do not want to look back and think if i had said this or that, it would have changed the outcome. i want to exhaust all of me for a chance to be with you. i know you don't believe i write for you. i will never give that away. if you could just ask yourself for me, if you had a dream, would you tell anyone you missed me? i have been giving humans i love space for a while now. i need closeness. i need permanence for once. i want to know if i loved you, would it matter as much to you as it does to me? what i am trying to say is, i want my next breath to be the one you just exhaled. i want to live and love under the moon with you. i want to know why your hands clinch when your eyes try and close. i want you naked with me when the sun catches us sleeping.

i knew when we met, i would never love anyone the same. there is no plausible explanation as to how or why i knew that, other than knowing your kiss would eventually become my undoing to all of the things i had experienced before you. humans speak of a holy tongue, a mouthpiece of a wild temptation and forgotten words. they speak of someone in future tense, with eyes deep blue and made from the ocean's lost graves. there is a treasure inside of what you call ordinary. there is a fire in what you call subtle. we knew there would come a day when goodbye was only saying hello in another life. there will be talks of this woman and where she lives and who she is. there will be birds building nests to hide your own words more when these days go behind my eyes. there is insanity in my actions, in my writings, in my active pursuit of what you mean to me. there could be a simpler way. an easier drift to take. i am not one for easy. if it isn't difficult or naive, it isn't for me. i have died a few times already. a few bones left in a salty and abandoned grave. a name written in sin, but still as bold as a red moon during a holy war. use your hands to teach me what the color of your soul is. all i see is yellow. all i feel is the moon. running my hand through your hair, i can feel the entire universe move with me. the earth learned how to walk the day you were born. you tell me you are high maintenance, but i will always love you as you are. you are maintaining your appearance and no one should ever tell a woman how to act, dress, or look. if she is willing to put forth the time and effort to love herself, you better take notice about how you treat her. a woman like her knows what she wants and won't shy away from letting you know how she feels. if you are looking for honesty, she fucking wears that, too.

there are humans who will cross your path at a moment in your own life where you thought nothing could ever have the courage to walk it to find you. where death sleeps in its grave and whispers in a hauntingly arrangement of sounds that you cannot help but listen to. where love is an erosion of self and only your decaying bones are left to fend for themselves. where light escapes all cracks, but pains you when it touches your remains. she brings me peace, a calmness only given to the ocean on a windless day out at sea, where kindness is a gentle wave helping you back to shore. she is my entire life's work that finally has a meaning. she is a soft gathering of humanity who awaits in anticipation for anything chasing after her. there is no running away to a new feeling. she will sit with it for hours around a fire and watch the flames speak to her in a way only the ash can attest to. she is the blue in my eyes and a decorated sunset upon the tops of every tree it touches and makes them stand taller to reflect its beauty. her name leaving my mouth never escapes without love attached to it in some way. she has seen more than most. she has lived more than many. it hasn't been easy for this adventuring woman made of comets and constellations. her hardships have yet to harden the flesh of moon she wears. she has her stories to tell. she has her words unsaid. she has her past that can be felt, but i am here for all of it. i am not a shallow swimmer and she knows it. we are both in the deep end of every body of water we can find. there is something sexy about the way she thinks. you can see her mind going over every aspect of life and it is right before her mouth opens to express herself that you see a thousand suns light up in her eyes. i do not believe in chance, luck, or happenstance. our souls hold energy from a million years ago. they have messages to tell each other if we are open to listening to someone who has traveled lifetimes to meet us. i believe in deep conversations, transparency, conviction of spirit, and a blood thirsty love that means no harm to either the heart, mind, or body. i simply want more of her; her time, her talks, her brimful laugh. at the end of the day, i value simplicity over anything else, yet she is the furthest thing from it. a kind of beauty like hers would take me light years to explain. you either feel it or you don't. and i feel her becoming a heart for my own to learn from.

i once told you the devil was a lie, then you smiled
back and told me you believed me. there is more
to you than my eyes can hold at times. there is
more to you than my body can embrace at times.
you have always been where i have needed you.
love is a common conception when shared by
common senses. what we make from it is up to
us, and i am not going to allow a day to go by
without telling you why and how i love you.
it is more important to me than words and
actions. it is a souly thing. it is bonely thing.
it is beneath the earth and inside of dreams.
it is beyond the blue moon and red skies. it is
something more than arms can hold back and
hide. you have always been more than a woman
to me. you have always been the ending to anything
i ever wanted it to look like when that day comes for
me. i will never tire of you. i will always be interested
in what you have to say, even if it takes you a little
longer these days to tell me. underneath a million
stars or a million cloudy days, it is you and i in this
life. i want to marry every piece of you. i want to be
engaged to every thought you come up with. you are
the light of night, piercing the moon herself. never
mistake my hands not being in yours for not wanting
you. they will always find you. they will always be in
spaces you leave open for me. tonight i will go to
bed and get to hold onto the only thing in this life
i will ever need in order to know if i am still alive.
your shine becomes the brightest when you say
everything with only your eyes.

i am after a love that can withstand a storm that has knocked out most of who i am. i am still yearning for a closing. i am still learning what you meant when you told me, "now just isn't a good time for us." i have let out all of the love inside of me and still no one is there to accept it. my solitude is becoming suffocating, but i am able to breathe, knowing your hand still holds mine. i miss the days when it was just you and i, and nothing stopping us from closing a distance we never thought could catch us. i can still sit here and laugh at the thought of making you smile, while doing nothing more than telling you how beautiful the day is because of the shine in your eyes. it kept me in the light more times than darkness had its hands around my throat. love me still. love me holy and unholy. love me and my moving parts that never knew how to settle for anything. i feel as if i am rolling over every rolling stone, collecting the dreams they left behind in their small towns. i feel as though i am backing down a flight of stairs where the exit is closed off just as my eyes are, thinking of you and how much i fucking miss you. i am in a room where the view is breathtaking, but all i can think about is picturing you on the bed and calling my name to interrupt the deathly silence between my ears. there are days i feel as though i will find someone else, then i remember my soul belongs to you. it is difficult to move on when your body no longer houses the same entity that got you here in the first place. i am trying. godammit, i am trying. i know how happy you are now, or at least i think you are. i think about the one you chose and left me for. it adds more incentive to find someone else for myself, but here i wait.

you deserve someone who wants to know why you scream out the lyrics to your favorite songs when they come on, the books you keep on the table beside your bed, and the reason why tears seem to form most when it is quiet. you deserve someone who will not judge your past, hold you when you cannot see yourself the way they do, and see value in scars you have been given over the years. you deserve someone who cares to ask you why you have earmarked certain pages and what you are afraid of, so they will know how to give their best effort in protecting you from it all. there are no perfect humans walking amongst us, but if we provide someone the ability to sleep in peace, live fully, and feel appreciated, we are living the best example of perfection. you deserve answers to tough questions, truth instead of blatant lies, and hands that never go without touching you. if what you are asking is too much for someone, they are incapable of giving what it takes to have you. it isn't your fault and you do not have high standards. you are simply tired of bullshit and want someone who is accountable and values the same things you do in a relationship. life is nothing more than choices, and i hope you are able to make one when you are ready to share that piece of your heart kept under your bed which only gets brought out when your eyes refuse to close. never settle just because it feels right. settling causes animosity and negative energy you want nothing to do with. it will end up poisoning you down the road. you deserve someone who understands all of this and still wants to kiss you each morning with eyes that have missed you. life is such a beautiful gift. until we appreciate it for what it is, instead of what is not, we will always live behind the light. stay true to your calling. find simplicity to be a magical sensation where breath meets a dream calling out its name. we are the chasers of a sun and moon who both knows us when we have difficulty knowing ourselves.

maybe i have forgotten what feelings are. maybe i have lost track of time and left too much darkness to fill in by myself. maybe i have forgotten everyone too soon without it being out of love. when i see you, my demons die. the devil breaks its own heart over the goodbye coming. when i see you, i see the rest of my life as i had hoped it would be one day. you smile as if you have never heard someone tell you how beautiful you are. you laugh as if you have never been hurt or left behind for someone else. you cry as though happiness is still something you long for, even when love sleeps in your heart and only opens its eyes to see the moon. my jaw has been hurting for years now, trying to swallow the earth that had been losing its way with what it thought would be okay in the end. but we are all strange birds. we are all our own temple of wicked torture and games to be played when left alone for too long by ourselves. though i must say, you are getting the best version of myself since the day i was born. ever since then, i have been involved with death and a tragic sense of wandering. i used to walk on my hands to read lines written by the road. there is a poet somewhere within me dying to get out and love you. dying to get out and write you the most beautiful set of words you have ever laid your eyes on. i know it hasn't been easy for you. just know it hasn't been roses and sunshine for me. it feels like i have been sleeping next to empty graves just to feel some sense of belonging. just to feel something that could hold me. now your hands hold mine. now your body holds my soul. now your smile reflects my light. it is the light you unearthed after you pulled the dirt out of my mouth. you are the one i have searched for. the one who almost gave up before i could reach you. you are my favorite sound. your laugh is my favorite color. your voice is the only reason i need to one day love you until the stars come down and collect us and the parts it gave us to shine a little brighter for others so we could find a way to say hello from a million miles away. there is no caution when it comes to certainty. you either run with it or jump from the fucking moon with only your convictions to save you. i am yours, just as the ocean is every soft movement before a wave is formed. you are the giant rise and nimble fall of my chest.

i'm not sure anyone will ever be you again. i want to believe
that will be a good thing. i want to believe you didn't mean
to break me into a million fucking pieces before you left me
for him. i want to believe you really did mean the words you
said to me each time we hung up the phone. i want to believe
it was only me the entire time and not you playing both sides
of a fine line you told me you needed to keep your mind safe
and your heart full. i want to believe you didn't steal a life i
had dreamt of since the first day you sent me a picture of
you on the beach, and told me, "this is to keep you warm."
devils come in all shapes and sizes. i just didn't know they
could ever get to me once you showed up. i want to believe
those early mornings where we got off the phone and you
went back to sleep and you did so without needing to tell
him the same thing. we once told told each other that we
would become ruined by the other. i simply thought you
meant it in a wholesome way. not in a way that would
make loving someone again this fucking impossible.
you took everything out of me and put it in the fire and
laughed at the flames. i want to believe you never meant to
hurt me in any way. but when i look back on it, i was the one
hurting myself by loving you when you weren't able to love me
back in the same way. you always told and talked to me about
actions. i was too blind to see the lack of effort you were giving.
i was too empty of a man to know the difference between love
and lack of self-control. i was only concerned about your
well-being. i was only worried about your life. i was caught up
in a world that never really got to love us back, because we kept
everything in house and away from those around us. i know it
wasn't all for nothing. my scars feel lighter today. the crosses
i had to carry are merely splinters i am picking out of my flesh.
though i am alone again, at least someone else can attempt to
break down walls you keep your love behind. i would have
done anything if you would have let me see your soul a little
more. i will only remember you for the sunset you were when
was looking for morning.

i never thought i would let someone else in again. i never thought
i would want someone to feel this familiar to me. i never thought
someone could kill the devil without them killing themselves.
but here you are, my sweet mercy. here you are before me, giving
me feelings i never thought could be possible. we talk as if our
friendship had been made on the star that created our souls.
we joke and kid around as if we have been in love before now.
as if my heart never had been broken before. as if yours had never
been bruised and punched out of your chest. i am giving you what
is left of a man the grave didn't take. i am handing over what is left
of a man that had been buried alive and left for the earth to eat from
the inside out. my hands reach out for you now. my eyes look across
these rooms full of humans to find you. though i know you will not
be found in person, your light still gives me hope i will find you when
it is time to hold you and make you understand how someone's body
is as close to a life needed as you will ever get. this ache haunts me,
but most of my best friends are ghosts these days. i am used to the
pain of loss and being without the love you need. i am used to
cussing at whatever moves just to get my aggression out without it
hurting me. i am not a monster like i was before when the alcohol
turned my skin green and i hated just the thought of breathing.
i am a kite in the hands of a child who is still learning how to fly
it without the wind. i am progress in retreat some days, but you,
my breathly light, you give me someone to run to. you give me
someone who isn't asking me to save them. you give me a clam
any hurricane would die for. i am not asking for more than you
can give me. i am not asking you to change anything about who
you are, because to me, beautiful is all i see and magic is all i feel.
you are bringing me back to love. it is the most intense, surreal,
and uncomplicated feeling i have ever felt. who would have
thought it needed to be that chaotic for me to find you in the
end. i have never went to bed, hoping for the sun to wake me
as quickly as i do now just to have a few minutes of dawn with
you before you go about your day. i have never known love to
have a name like yours. i have never felt more at ease with who
i am than i do with you. i think that is what life is about. it is
finding the dawn, the dusk, the rise and fall of light in someone
who loves to watch it with you. and you sit with them, craving
theirs just as badly; a symmetrical force.

to have gone through life, and now finally finding a reason
to be better, to be more human, to be more love than my
pain, it all gives me hope as the rain falls around me.
these storms have been crucial to my upbringing, to my
ability to dance when others feel their bones break under
thunder. i was once scared of myself. i was once afraid of
what i was capable of if pushed too far. the edge i was on,
was not for the weak. i balanced my heart and mind over it,
hoping one would eventually give up and all of us go over.
i have never felt worthy of much. i have always been to quiet
to find a scream within me. i have always been to brittle for
my own expectations. i have known more ghosts than
humans. i have known more loss than lost graves i would
walk over to feel a story they had to tell. i have gone through
multiple breakups and each one ended because i wasn't
enough or they lied when they told me a different reason.
but today, with you, i am not ashamed of anything in my life
or what i have done in order to survive. i am not scared of
your truth, your beauty, or your colorful ways of being who
you are. there is something new about you i haven't found
in anyone else, and that excites me and brings the stars i
have kept hidden in my own pockets of darkness. we all
have it. sometimes, it just takes someone brave enough to
walk it alone until they find yours to help them see how
much light actually lives in the corners of a forgotten
room. i am not into tracing body parts. i am after your
goddamn soul. i want to see what it looks like when we
are both standing there with nothing but our wounds to
show. with nothing but our scars to love. i know you will
be there for me in the end. i wouldn't have taken this
chance again. not after what the one before you did to
me. we are all deserving of someone who wants to love
us. who wants to be there. who chooses our story to stay
in. since you have been here, i have felt the earth shift,
the universe grow and change in my favor. maybe this
time it will be more. maybe this time it will last. i believe
in your ability to teach me your past so i can be in your
future. my broken will be loved again if this all falls apart.

this is me still trying to find truth about love, life, and all
the ache i feel throughout my day. this is my new chapter.
my new beginning. my endless attempt at breathing in
what is meant to stay and breathing out what never was.
if you look close enough, you can see the love in the
shadows. you can feel the warmth from a heart in the
things holding you. you can smell forgiveness coming
from the blooms around you. you can hear patterns
of a life opening and closing as you take your breath.
we stay connected to places we give our truths to.
you can go into your backyard and feel the same energy
as someone in california or new york. the same energy
from the beaches where waves continue to churn despite
the moon not having as much strength as it needs, but
fights on, because we all need love. the moon is never
not in love with who you are. she knows the love and
loss it takes to be whole and alive. she knows what it
takes when hiding half of who you are is all you can do
to make the ache go away. she still comes back stronger
than before. she is the shore of magic. we are the light
of love and all the wild from a moon's kiss to the stars.
keep dancing in the energy inside of you. stay as crazy
as you can about the things that move you from place
to place. from dream to dream. once we lose that, we
become what we have fought our entire lives not to be;
normal and without a spark of madness. in the quiet
moments, may love always speak in moonish ways.
may it keep your light safe and alive for the adventure
calling our names. may it lead us into a new day with
a new face. may we always look out into the sea and
find reasons to swim again. we are the waves returning
to shore. safely and homely, it all comes back restored.
take your time with love, your breath, and thought.
we are where we are supposed to be. even when the sun
sets differently. even when the moon becomes stranded,
we bring it all back to the place we need it most. our bones
have broken before, but not today. we are the reason for
today. we are the reason love still speaks with gentleness.

love never forgets a human who knows it to be the only thing needed in order to live forever. as much as we all hope for it, sometimes, it takes its time getting to us. sometimes, patience is love. regardless of moments passed, we are the lifeblood to every living thing we come into contact with. love is not the only thing. it is the undying day we all search for. we are the creators of magic, light, and all things hopeful. we are the catalyst for the universe to give us a miracle when all we have known are troubled waters. breathe in forgiveness for who you once were. breathe out an absolute purpose to become someone you needed before love found its way to you. we are the limbs and bodies of all our dreams. the ocean only knows depth. it only knows how to kiss the moon with a wave of its own waters. with the sound of crashing love against the bottom of her soul. we are from a place where we know the sounds she does, the colors baptized by fire and rock. by fate and chance running hand in hand together underneath her abiding love. nothing feels as good as knowing we are more than our broken. we are all free within our journey to the center of her blue. may you always be with closure, clarity, and the fiercest love imaginable. may it reignite your soul and take you places you have been held back from. may it give you a new dream to chase after with eyes opened or closed. we hold all of the answers. never question why you are still here. live the reason and perfect the act of being imperfect. someone who knows your path and the hell you have gone through will find you one day. you will see the ashes they continue to wipe from their face just as you have with your own.

i have been living life afraid and with uncertainty. i was raised to always believe in myself no matter the situation facing me. at times, it is hard to live up to that standard. at times, it is easier doing the minimum required of me. playing it safe and not exploring. waiting for something to happen instead of making shit happen for myself. i am human and most of what is going on in my head is self-induced. i am relearning who i am. i am relearning what i want. i am balancing life, work, and priorities now. it feels good being on top of your own mountain after settling for trails that kept me safe. explore and reach new goals. failing is only possible if you are trying. success comes shortly after. i am still capable of loving myself. i believe that is the greatest lesson i have learned. regardless of how dark and lonely it gets in my head, i know i have found what i needed while being on this journey. i am more lost than ever before in many ways, but at least i can speak honestly about it. lost is a home i carry with me. i have matured into the wanderer i have always wanted to be. with or without anyone else, i know who i am. some days it scares me. other days it brings me life. you taught me how to make a decision and stay true to it. you taught me how to sacrifice things you once could not live without in order to achieve my desires. being here has shown me how much i never actually needed you beyond the point of which we got to. but i am thankful nonetheless for your love, guidance, and resiliency to shape me into the man i am today.

you are going to be my greatest poem, my greatest form
of power and release. i am going to love you until we are
breathless, until our fucking souls give out and give up
on the chase of something more than what we have.
there is nothing and will be nothing left of you except a
pile of stars where you once stood before me; naked and
willing to take on the universe with me. you are bones i
wish to lay with once my flesh has departed who i am and
gone back to where it all began. i will write you in every
way i can, keeping you safe and holding you like a breath
being kept by a secret we share. i am going to give you
what is left of me and my life. wherever the light finds
me, i know you will be the reason why it stays longer
than it should. you are a moonish love, a soulful delight
of passion and rage. a beautiful bounty laces through
each kiss i press onto your skin. hands weaving in and out
of your hair, then back to your throat where i gently press
and firmly hold to let you know i am needing a little
more. you are an angel's heartbeat, with a devil on both
shoulders. my eyes are watching both to see who turns
away first. you will be someone i carry around with me
often. a memory like this is one i used to have before
you. one where i would lay in a coffin, hoping it would
stay open long enough to see something else to live for,
before darkness took me away. the earth wasn't ready
for me yet. the universe forgot my name and allowed me
a second chance after my third attempt at love. i have no
idea where we will end up, but as long as you are close to
me, it gives me enough strength to never give up on what
it is we are after. i am too old for happy ever afters. i am
too old for happy endings. i know neither hardly ever
happen, but maybe, just maybe, being fucking in love
with you will give me enough breath to be alive more
than ever before. i am not looking for a fairy-tale. i am
wanting to take you home and love on you for the rest
of my life. i have no vows. i do not believe in marriage.
i simply believe in two souls finding love within two
humans and making it work until two becomes one.

i still have to remind myself to slow down with you. i know how strong i can be when it comes to feelings i cannot find words for. i know my soul well enough to know when it has become a chaotic mess of emotions, mixed with art escaping a wild pull from yours. she wears her bruises and shares her scars with the moon at night when silence finds them in a thought. she's the universe with an infinite way about her looks. beautiful could be said, but i simply stare and have nothing perfect to say, so i shut my mouth and appreciate the way her light shines onto me. i am more to her than i have ever been with anyone else. i am more of myself than i have ever been before in my own life. she has been told how precious she is, but she has heard it too many times to believe it now. she has been told how well in-tune she is with the stars, but she can barely hold darkness most of the time. she has a difficult time believing in her own love. the way life has taken away so much of the girl she was while growing up too fast to count only a handful of birthdays she actually remembers, makes me want to celebrate her every goddamn day. someone like her deserves to be cherished, to be seen, to be heard for the way the sun rises again to show her someone cares. she has been sending me sunsets and all i can give her are words that can match colors she makes. i am still getting used to a slow approach. i have always been a runaway train slamming into city walls and breaking through barriers i put up to keep myself from falling too fast for someone i barely know. she's got sacrifice in her voice. you can feel each splinter she speaks with. the frost has left the cold and i have stopped shaking. my shivers have become the calmest of waves with her arms nestled and entwined with mine. a nebulous has left me and i am clear to the bone with a touch of love these days. when she calls out to me, my inner child comes back home. she is nature to me, all of its beauty is defined by her way of looking at trees dance in the wind just for her. she has this way of keeping out the noises in my head and turns them into a whisper to silence anything that doesn't belong there. she's a mercy i have cried out for. i no longer have to fight anymore. she remains undefeated when it comes to my demons. i have yet to find words, but she is beautiful to me.

there were places on the map we never got to, but love found us before we were ready. it is still here, still breathing, still able to linger longer than a star can shine. a life means nothing if you aren't prepared to spend it fighting for every fucking thing you cannot live without. so here i am, without you, but maintaining my purpose with a fire to get back to you and the moon within you. maybe if i keep wandering, i will find you watching the same sunset. your pillow talk was my favorite language and things are incredibly quiet now. i am used to my silence, but yours is something i will never get used to. the patterns of life are monotonous at times. our imaginations create and build images of who we need to be. looking past the glass of the human it reflects, there is a wildfire of monumental strength. a kind with a raging force that will engulf the untraveled maps of our universe. my sky is still beautiful without your colors. each afternoon i can find your eyes staring at me, wondering if i am thinking about you. the birds show me. the trees show me. the still breeze sits with me and explains how much a human can miss the wind once you have to use your hands to keep yourself from falling on your fucking face. there is so much i would like to say to you, but you already know how i feel. sometimes, that is all there is. more words left until someone comes along and actually cares what you have to tell them.

there was a sun and he loved the moon very much. they spent lifetimes apart, but found each other in the sky every day and night. each year passed and they got closer together. the stars would celebrate each passing day by shining their lights towards them. they cheered on love and wanted happiness. one day, they touched each other and were given a million more opportunities to figure out how to survive once the storms came in. they kept fighting and would do anything for the other. a journey is a constant endeavor for all that you will need. no matter how you get there, do not allow people to second guess you or pretend they know what kind of a struggle it has been for you. they will say things. they will do things. maybe it was because of them you started. hopefully, it was because of what you wanted for yourself. there's no greater victory in this world than conquering your own mind. roam this wild landscape until you become all you will ever need. it was a lesson the sun and moon learned together. they knew what was in front of them, but they knew love was greater than any other reason others would come up with as to why it wouldn't work. they both shine for an eternal jubilation. they both love incessantly, despite a struggle they are both fully aware of. we all go through our battles of doubt. it gets easier once you realize doubt is just a part of love we suppress once our hearts speak for us, instead of someone else's opinion.

i never prayed to find you, because god never saw
me to begin with. i have been on my own and in
my own spiritual world since before we met.
i needed you to know that before we got any
further away from who we are at this very moment.
you need to know the truth about me and my beliefs.
i come from a place where gods do not survive too
long without killing mortals. i come from a place
where stars replace humanity. i come from a place
where love actually turns out to be enough and
makes anything understand the wrong that has
been done to it. i am no better than anyone you
have met. i do not offer precious metal or money.
i do not offer any type of reward for making it last
with me. i am nothing but honesty with a heart
that has cared for my own scars longer than any
other human ever thought about staying to see
where the beginning and end of them are on my
body. love is a wild thing, a strange thing, a terrible
fucking excuse to kiss an ache. but it still listens
and clutches a constant courage to go deeper
than the root of my pain. lay with me, tell me
your story about how you got your wings and
how you learned to speak about unearthly
things. i will tell you every goddamn secret
i sleep with and keep hidden underneath the
moon. once you trust me, you will have the love
of every moon above you. you will have her full
attention as you do with my own. i will love you
until love decides to let us embrace a sweet
victory of honey and gold.

love still keeps me safe even if it no longer knows my name the way you did. my own idea of what it still can be for me keeps it all from floating above and out of my chest. i have still kept some for myself. i have still kept some just for fun. days and nights all run together now. it is difficult for me to tell the sun and moon apart, but i know all light and energy remain the same. one day i won't look for you to help me or get me out of my mind. i am still a wanderer at the end of the day, so that is what i lean on now instead of promises you made to keep me standing tall. my love still sleeps with me even if a bed cannot keep me made. some days i wish you would call, but that would keep me going backwards on a train that won't turn around to see your tracks. my body still has your smell on it. i can close my eyes and tell you exactly where you touched me today. the lightly pressed fingerprints of your soul still shine through me and my demons. each one dies a little more as my breath fades and finds a new reason to breathe. there is this woman i am in love with, but i will give you a guess as to why we aren't together. time and space does wonders for someone looking for more of it, but it will remain the main reason why i am going to sleep alone for the millionth time tonight. i have stared death in the face and walked past it as if it didn't know my name. an encounter like that is something you do not ever forget. it stays with you and makes you want so much more from life. knowing how close you were to an ending, makes you appreciate and value every beginning from that point forward. my life is changing all for the better. i honestly had no idea where i would be a few years ago. today it is raining and cloudy, though i swear i have never seen so much light before. when i was younger, i would hear people say, if you wish for the little things to happen, then you will receive them. now i understand that is is true. grow with the flowers and trees around you. learn how it takes time to complete sentences of life. i am finally taking my first step again. a step towards building something incredibly special with you. a breath with you is something worth fighting for. a breath with you, keeps the life in me from leaving my dreams.

the moon still knows us and loves us even though love is absent at this moment. you were made for greater things. you were made for a love that never fails to meet you where stardust turns to aspirations. where dreams go to slip into something more comfortable and takes you into a new reality. music sings and adds a different shade of human to my sighs. my clothes are feeling looser today. maybe i am losing weight or finally removing everything that once made me perfect for you. wherever this love and loss takes me, i can only hope we are given one more chance to prove to a cosmos it wasn't out of place or wrong when it paired our souls together before flesh became our home. my hands miss yours. my eyes miss yours. my entire life misses you, but i cannot tell you that, because you have found someone new to miss when you are alone. i can still remember every phone call we made to each other. the times we hung up because the other had to go still leaves me speechless and out of breath, gasping and grasping for one more hello to come through and change our goodbyes. we will see each other gain very soon. either on this side of the moon or the other.

i am finally coming to terms with your letting go.
i have bruises that still look like you. i still have
a heart that is trying to erase and clean out the
room you were staying in. love makes us all a
bit messy. it leaves us all a little fucked up
and feeling heavy after your bones decide to
leave a home it once built to keep it all from
coming down around you. i am not better
without you as you have told me before,
but i know if i don't learn how to move
on, i am going to miss everyone who wishes
to stay with me, should i ever make it that far.
my life is at a standstill, a hover above wounded
graves. my life is full of misused objects i thought
would end up decorating who it was i thought
myself to be. you are still a breath in these lungs,
lying to fresh air around it, telling it how life can
go on. i thought i saw you today. she looked just
like you and the way she twirled her hair, had my
fingers moving with hers. i couldn't find the
bravery to ask her what her name was, so i left
and wrote about a woman i will never know but
fell in love with. it seems as though that is about
par for me these days. thinking i have proper
acumen, when in fact, that too, has gone missing
and has been replaced by a sweet fucking misery
that looks a lot like you.

i know there is a struggle you cannot speak of, but without its
haunting, you would not be you. i know your eyes are tired of
not being able to close when night beckons your soul to rise.
i know exhaustion is not something you love to wear, but
your art has a beautiful mind and anyone can see its magic
and shine. you touch the canvas of any living thing and
connect a heart to a human without thinking of anything
else but bringing home the lost in each and every one of us
you call upon for inspiration. you are gentle with each breath.
it is why the moon rises for you. you are a woman of purpose.
it is why the colors find you before you can use their name to
paint with. there is life inside of you, wild and true to form.
you may not see yourself the i do or those around you view
you, but i promise, there is a majestic quality in humans that
can call on the night to bring out its stars. you have changed
my life. you have changed the way i write. you have changed
the color of my blood from red to purple, from orange to
blue. we are nothing of sorts in this life. we are nothing a
label changes. we are nothing more than artists trying to
find the right words, the right angles, the right way of going
about making life mean more than just waking up and pouring
out what we were born with. i do not know anything about you
other than the lovely way you captivate the sun and capture a
face with beauty only you can see. i know life has been anything
but easy for you, but i have a feeling your talents are going to
take you well beyond your dreams. well beyond any time and
space that could ever hold you. you are a friend, and i needed
to remind you just how fucking rare it is to have something or
someone like that in this ungodly life. i know it hasn't been the
world you thought you would be living in, but i am thankful
each day i open my eyes to see you are still here. to see you are
still creating something more than art. you are creating hope
for many just like me. without you, the details would be blurry
and the earth would be colorless. you are the art many of us
hope to make someday come to life. you are the whisper many
of us need to keep going, to keep living, to keep loving, even
after the story is done with us.

there was a love with us that could have been fire without the rain. we were still trying to get through the pain that found us once we left out our names and forgot our faces. we were something more than the flesh told us we were. love knew us by our hearts, by the ways the moon would kiss us before our eyes fell behind our darkness. we are what happens when everything we believe in becomes the same thing that keeps us from being more, because of the way we relaxed by our bones. i could tell you anything you wanted to hear, but you always had a way of only hearing yourself once i got too close. love is still shaking out the thunder and stroking out the lightning crashing down around us. where you stand is where i once laid my feet, hoping i would be able to stand. though these days, my back is horizontal with the horizon we made out of broken things and lost stars. we were dreamers, you and i. once you awake from a story you never saw an ending to, you can only stay long enough to see how it kills you at the end by telling and showing you nothing matters if your love cannot withstand the shattered glass from windows you once kept open to see a sunrise. my life was you, so forgive me if i am finding it difficult, almost damn near impossible to find my way out this place. my limbs weigh me down with a mercy only known to gods who have wasted their gifts on humans. i am a misplaced soul now, without a home to retreat to. i will sit here until the sunset gives me a new color to chase and a new woman to forgive me for not being saved by a god she may still believe in after finding me the way she did.

love is love, regardless of who and where we find it in. life is made up of a million unknowns dancing with a hidden meaning behind every step we take. be aware of those who latch onto more than you can give. be fully aware of the stress we take on in order to secure whatever feeling we summon to protect who we are. there is magic in healing. there is magic in a fire we sit with and keep adding a spark to keep it alive. we are all starving to taste a sacred emotion, an endless attempt of drowning for a love we believe can save us in the end. we must find common ground to stand on or else we will fall and crumble with mountains which once gave us hope to rise again. we must give our hearts a chest that can hold its colors and promises. we are the givers of night, of light, of a passing glance that may save a life if we believe in it. i have been trying to learn how to be better by watching flowers in a breeze during summer. they sway and swing with conviction to hold onto each petal for as long as they can. their roots bring me to attention for their strength during storms and their acrobatic ingenuity. i mirror the day, the feeling, the need to find closure. i am an opened carcass, exposing every bone i have broken trying to save remaining parts of a love i left for someone who will plant me and care for me. one day the sun will shine again and will know peace, just as a butterfly passes my eyes and never blinks. finally finding my way after you left has been the most unexpected exit that has ever greeted me. i am still in the infant stages of moving on. i haven't changed much about who i am. at least we did something right together.

i have heard stories about a creature who sleeps with the moon in his bed and never goes hungry for love. light travels a long way once you have been in love with darkness your entire life. things feel foreign after you have touched a devil's idea. you begin to question it all, as if you were finally able to see hell for what it is, instead of being trapped inside of it. we love to release. we love to let go. we love to love. we are all human at the end of the day and it is our duty to pursue every single fucking thing that catches our souls on fire. we are after the next chase, the next adventure, the next forever. love will always know us, even if death reaches us first. there is a small bit of light left for us if we are willing and ready to go after it instead of putting our hands over our eyes, pretending everything is okay when we know better. the creature in us and with us, understands our days and eyes better than anyone else. i will keep sleeping with the moon. i will keep her close to the only vacant room i have left in my heart to share, to give, to render. i am nothing more than a few hundred scars plastered against bone with a name that is still beginning a dream, a movement. until i am ready to let go completely, i am cursed by angels and displaced by demons. i am nothing more than a few hundred lines of cocaine waiting on a human to put aside and throw away eventually. my addictive personality only gets me so far until a current high wears off and i am in search for a fresh face that can see me without needing me to guide their hands around my scars. humans tell you they want it all, but i have learned they love lying more when it comes to your past and life's brands it marked you with.

i can see where the stars get their shine from, where they get their hope from. i walked away from you before i knew who you could be for me, but i will remember what you did for me. there will always be a closeness i feel with the night because of who you are to me. ever since you have been gone, i have tried relentlessly to change the color of my eyes to see you better, to see you clearer. i have failed miserably at it, but i am too young to forget my old ways. love may never know me like it did before i met you, and that is what i hope happens before i fall apart trying to piece back together what you dropped on purpose. my sense of everything is tired and lonely. i am a forgotten prophet who has gone into hiding to stage his own victory where sea meets shoreline. there is forgiveness in the shape of your smile. there is hope in the form of your hands touching broken parts of me still too fragile for others to gather. i will manage to get through this. i will confide my secrets within a moonish wish. maybe one day you will understand a lie i tell you to be the absolute truth in the life ahead of this one we lost together. i said i didn't love you, but it was only to protect me from what i am feeling now without you. it was never meant to hurt you. i was merely sacrificing today for the next fifty years of possibly waking up to a clean conscious. when you told me you were leaving your life behind to begin a new one, i had no idea you were getting rid of me along with it. i guess all devils know what they want after hell releases their souls back into the world. i guess all lovers meet a tragic death once you take the gun out of your mouth to see who would pull the trigger first. sometimes we forget the weapon is loaded and our hearts have no remorse for cowards who blink at the opportunity to love again.

some days i am okay with everything in my life. other days
i curse the names of everyone who has ever done anything
to hurt me. i am okay with anger being a reason to be
alive. it drives me most days. it dictates what goes and
who stays in my life. i talked to my dad today about my
anxiety. he is old school and never really talks about his
own struggles, but ever since we were kids, he has kept
an open line of communication with my brothers and i.
i told him last night i was laying in bed and in my head,
i kept hearing, "you are going to die. you are going to die.
you are going to die." for over an hour it was on a loop
on top of all the other things i have done in my life.
every fucking bad thing strikes me down when the
moon goes into hiding. the demons come after me
with their pitchforks and fire. i turn over and see the
first time i lied to someone and how emotionally scarred
they were because of it. i turn to the other side and see
how many times i hurt my parents because of my actions
or lack there of. i lay on my back and see every hell and
devil i have faced since i was a little boy fighting for
his fucking life. my anxiety is deathly. it is messy. it isn't
for any other human to consume. i am afraid of it, but
i know it isn't something that will kill me. the shakes,
the dizzy spells, the million miles an hour overthinking.
it all meets me head on when i go to bed. my dad told
me he was sorry i was going though it. i know if it gets
any worse, i will go to the doctor and get medication.
i am not ashamed of needing them if that is what it
takes. i am not ashamed of speaking public about this.
maybe someone needs to hear that someone else feels
this way so another life can make it. mental health
needs a bigger platform. i will stand on fucking
mountains, yelling from the top of my lungs until
more are able to speak openly about it. my anxiety
could be a cure for someone else's. i will protect it
at all costs. this is me. this is my life. there is nothing
perfect to see or hear here. i am just a human trying to
love again and find someone that can love me for trying.

i am not scared of many things these days. i have seen
death up close and its touched my face without me
moving or stepping back. the only time i flinched,
was when i tried to end my own life because my
thoughts couldn't be helped. i am a free man and
no longer a prisoner to my soul and its demons that
roam the isolated land inside of me. though some days
i can feel the cuffs, i can still feel the ropes and binding
forces. i speak without pause in my throat. for once you
have come face to face with your own pain, you learn how
glorious it is to embrace the ache for what it is and what it
is trying to teach you. i am still afraid of love. i am still
afraid of what it has taken away form me. i am still scared
i may never know it again. if you were to ask me what
scares me the most, that would be it. maybe this is as
close as we will get. maybe this is as close as you will let
me wander with you. i would give anything to touch you.
not in a sexual way, but a reassuring kind of way. the kind
of touch that gives a year meaning. the kind of touch that
gives loneliness a place to go. the kind of touch that
releases a soul to go back to a home it was once forced
to vacate. all i know is how to move on my feelings,
my urges, my desires to be as close to you as love was
intended to be. i have been afraid of dark rooms and
moonless nights, but not with you here by my side.
we barely know each other because of distance, though
i would move all of heaven and hell just to make it
easier to get to you. i have seen humans destroyed
because of that word. i will always hope whatever we
are, whatever we become, gives us a chance to love
until death is just another word we give a new meaning
to. you are the muse, artist, woman, and human i will
forever look to when it becomes evident i cannot do
anything but think of you. our eyes will forever connect,
because we know the truth they speak with. we know
where they go when they close for the night.

i have mistaken love for something that lasts, but this mistake brought
me you. at its worst, love is still everything to someone who has been
fooled by a devil and its demons. i have been running around in circles,
trying to burn out the sun. i have been doing all i can to keep any light
away from me and my darkness. i never thought anyone would want
what was left of a man buried by his own hands. you have come into
my life with a new moon, a new approach to breathing. i haven't
even met you yet, but when a soul is moved by someone you barely
know, all you can do is move your body with it. i have been left on
the pavement, searching for any signs of life, while my past plays
with my eyes, tricking them into looking for what i am without.
the years i have lived prior to us meeting have no idea of your
capabilities. slowly, we are getting there, and i am doing all i can
to tell you who it is you are talking to. life and love are both ghastly
when it is being led with uncertainty. i look at you and see fifty
years flash before me. i see every part of me wanting to be something
more for you. i will never go a day without telling you how rare and
beautiful you are. i will never go a day without telling you, thank you,
for allowing me to share this space with you, to share a breath with
you. i have been lonely half my life. i have been a loner, but by
choice. when you came into my world, i knew i would choose to
move forward with you. i knew i needed your smile, your laugh,
your insane ability to love me and my brokenness. the pieces are
not always heavy. i simply have trouble with the walking and acting
as if i am okay. i have a difficult time admitting to things when i
honestly do not feel a conviction to do so. i know i will spill out
my indies if it means you understanding what i have been eating to
survive, to see the bullshit i have been fed and made to think was
healthy by someone who said it was. i have been nameless and
faceless for years now. even when love knew me, i had no fucking
clue what it looked like when it was a part of my life, when it was
a part of me. my hands are swords some days when i am typing.
i am defensive. i am hardened. i am cold. i am ruthless. growing
up, i had to be. being in war, i had to be. fighting cowards, i had
to be. fighting my own mind, it was necessary. i cannot wait to
go to sleep with you, as i am holding the next lifetime in my
arms. i cannot wait to wake up with you and tell you all about
the dreams i had. i cannot wait to kiss you and tell you how
long i have waited to touch your flesh with them. i cannot
wait to be someone better for you, for myself, because that
is what and who you are to me.

i'm still trying to make up for all of the bad i have done. all of the bad
still left in me from my addictions, my past, my lack of any control for
love and what love has done to me. humans in my circle think they
know me, but still do not understand my yearning for self-expression,
my tattoos, my religious views, my art, my scars, all of which are still
an unknown to them. i can feel and sense their judgment long
before a word is said. it is one of the many perks of being an empath.
my sarcasm still loves me at least. they will never see me as i see myself,
and that will forever be a blessing and a curse. for them not to know
my pain, but read about it, then them asking me why i don't talk about
it with them, is beyond heartbreaking for me. it is the sword i have put
down during many of battles at this point. i honestly don't know if my
immediate family will ever know me, but it pains me to think they
have an idea as to who i am. i am working on me now. i have no
control over how others view me. i have no control over what they
see or what they want to believe. this year has taught me to do more
of what i want and less of what others think i should do. i am ashamed
it has taken me this long to figure out that part. so many of my friends
have left this earth without knowing who i was or what they meant to
me. when i was twenty years old, i lost someone i loved dearly. she was
a few years younger than i was, but over that summer, we kept in touch
and almost began dating. when i returned from connecticut, i went
back home and she was at a party we were hanging out at. i wanted
her to stay with me and be with the rest of us, but she got into a car.
that was the last time i saw her alive. she died that night. today marks
thirteen years since she passed away. well, two days after to be exact.
i knew then how cruel love and life would be for me down the road.
i knew it long before then, but it was the punch in the soul others
had spoken about when they had told me life wasn't fair. i think of
death too often and would make others incredibly uncomfortable
with my thoughts on it. it is fucking maddening when all you want
to do is love and be loved. maybe we never get a chance to be in
love again after the first one slips through our cracks. i think how
endearing it is to have someone love you in this fucked up world.
how it can save you if you let it in. it is why i never go a single day
without telling those i love, just how much i love them. it is why
i am so fucking passionate about love. maybe one day i can find
someone like that again. someone who is just as fucking crazy
about it as i am.

i wanted you to see the sun this morning. i wanted you to
see the moon last night. i kept waiting for you, but you never
showed. my hands grew weary and my feet turned into water,
as i slowly drowned in my own ocean. i kept my head above
it all just long enough to see you come by. i yelled for you,
but you kept walking as i said goodbye. a humming bird
visited me today and taught me how to use my arms to fly
and remain above the thing it wanted most. i watched it as
it left, so gentle with magic and soft with its light. i wondered
what kept you from me. i thought about it for a while after
i caught my breath. after all of the water had drained from
me, nothing but salt was left. i thought you had been in your
own ocean, in your own house of horrors. i didn't blame you
for hearing what you wanted instead of my screams. i think it
worked out best for the both of us, for you and me. i am doing
better now. i rest my head on the shore and don't take on
water. i slide my hands into the sand and pull out shells and
treasures that had washed up from the wreckage i was once
before. i look at myself with baby eyes and a tender heart.
i look at who i am now and finally see myself. when all of this
is over, when all is said and done, all wars will be over and the
battles will have been won. my life has no room for cowards
and fakes, for liars and energy thieves. the lions roar, kill,
and roam with an intense wild. my ravens fly with the black
of night and no remorse for picking off the weak and eating
what is left of the ending beyond me. my weapons are cleaned
and put away. my words i use to curse with are still being
prepped. one step for me, is a step i never could have taken
without you. my heart leads an army and my soul leads its
own nation. my love is an instrument i will play and call on
when the timing is right, right before the doves come calling
home for the dawn. i think i wanted you because something
about you made me feel safe, complete, maybe a little more
human than death had led me to believe. i want different
things now. i want love to not be anything more than it
needs to be; free from falling, free from rising. tonight,
i have a bear in my best and hibernation is over. tonight,
i have a sweet love beside me who keeps me warm when
the fire goes out and the stars blush at who we are.

XO

i sat down here before i was ready to tell you how i felt. i wish i could tell you how i felt. i wish i could see you and everything be okay between us. i wish i could see you and you be as happy to see me as i would be to hold you. but i know that is a pipe dream, a few hundred pennies down a wishing well. i was crazy before i met you, and now, i have lost my head completely. walking around with a lost love inside of you may be the most painful experience one can hold when it comes to a heart already breaking from separation. once you begin separating from your body, that's when living becomes dreaming with your eyes open. it is why i have a hard time sleeping most nights. it is why i have a difficult time paying attention to anything that doesn't remind me of you. you would think i would be better by now. you think i would be okay by now. the truth is, i have no fucking idea what better is or if i ever was such a word to begin with. i think i have always been lost to a cause greater than what i could fit into my body. i walk around as if the pain is tolerable, but i just play the part medicine cannot give to me. i am stubborn when it comes to you. i know i should turn around and forget you ever existed. i know i am breaking my chest open daily to make sure you are still inside. i don't know how to not feel you, so i do what i know how to do. i write you out, one feeling at a time. one unforgettable moment at a time.

i have been wondering how long i would have to be without you, without a feeling of needing to be any closer than this. i have kept my hands to myself and have only been able to type about you for the last few months without gritting my teeth in remembrance of pain. i have been at this desk, wondering how long i could in fact type about you without falling in love with you again. it is a thought i have been chewing on for years now. i can still see you as you were before i met you. you were a sweet light in the sky, a smiling face with a kind and gentle touch for helping broken humans in need of love. you have always been a reminder to those looking, if you search long enough, all of the gold will be there in the end. it will be right where they told you it would be. i wonder too often these days. i wonder what will become of me if i remain here without anything else but my words to use when no one else can understand my thoughts. i wonder away with kindred and spiritual thoughts of a future which keeps me busy planning the next five years of my life. i could go on for another twenty-five years attempting to hash out plans, but i am a man who only has today to make love with, to make sense with. to make anything i feel, not feel as if i am removing knives and swords from my back and heart. i never could tell you how sorry i was for saying what i did to you. you didn't deserve that side of me. life tends to make us all evil if given enough time. life tends to make us all devils if we have enough time to tear the wings away and replace them with our intentions. i could write about you for the rest of my life, and i believe i am going to. once you fall in love with someone who sees your scars and shows you theirs, love finds a way to heal your entire life. there is no masking what is scorched and seared on your soul, but they make it less of an obstacle and more of an event to celebrate, because you survived this version of hell. you are a million quiet thoughts. you are a half-read book, because something else took your attention away. you are the warmest spot in the room. you are someone who pushes their luck, because you have always made your own. i was in love with you then and i remain in love with you now. it will be that until my last breath comes out as your name. i am cursed by it, but it is something i will love and continue to enjoy, because my curse is my most beloved blessing. all miracles are endearing once you understand not every one of them tends to serve you for your present. some stay long after only to reveal to you that beauty remains in the absence of what you thought you needed.
you are still love to me.

there is no better love than yours. humans tell each other
everything they wish to hear, but never believe in for
themselves. i wish you could see it. i wish i could tell you
how grand you are and how magic is still around. but you
stopped believing in that shit years ago. long before i showed
up. long before winter stole your smile and shine. i woke up
this morning with my soul still attached to yours in the fight
for breath and victory. for ample reason to suggest anything
else matters. nothing else does if it isn't you. i am losing sleep.
i am losing memories of who you are and what you did for me.
i just wish i could lose the ones of what you did to me. but the
devil loves to play match maker with you and your demons.
it loves to come between your sanity and that little piece of
peace you once found in someone else. i know it will be
alright. i know this feeling of demeaning will leave. i know
pain can last until the ground takes back what it gave to you.
i know love can last until the universe takes back who you were
before the flesh made you powerless. defeat isn't the end for me.
i have too many reasons why it will be okay, even if you aren't
one of them anymore. i used to tell you how much i loved you.
i used to tell you to just hold me for a little while. my arms are
capable of doing it now. when before, they remained another
motionless attempt at surviving what i was never fully prepared
for. i may come up short in a lot of situations where someone
else is favored, but i will make this one count. i have more to
prove, but none to you. once someone becomes the moon,
you have to eventually look for the stars to lead you home.
though you will be up there, my eyes will periodically slide
over to watch you to see if you can still radiate like before.
i will just remind myself it isn't for me anymore. it isn't my
phase to rush or care for. we are givers and takers, but today,
i am just another poet trying to make sense of loss and love.

tell me something, whisper it to me slow. i need to remember what it feels like to feel again. i need to feel what it is like to be with love again. i am not afraid of my own face. i am not afraid of lonely spaces between this place and yours. i am a wild thought caught inside of a mind that is too much chaos and not enough time to process the purchase of an idea. i am calling out to you. why can't you hear me? why can't you take a second to look at me and see i am alone with a feeling of an uneasy temptation. there are humans walking these streets that will never know me. there are humans walking these streets that will never again have a warm meal to eat. i look at my hands and the coffee it picked up and remember life isn't bad at all. it is just the mind that fucks with me and makes me less of a man at times. it is what scared me being with you. i think deep down i would always feel that with you. my mind never allowed me peace before you, which is why it was incredibly difficult losing you. you brought me my life back. you brought me the capacity to try love again. to try life again. my mind is still searching for self-love. i know one day i will find it and be who i need to be in order for someone to stick around and make something meaningful together. i think solitude is healthy for anyone looking for reminders. i have been in it for so long, i have forgotten the feel of another human being staying for more than a day, a month, longer than i can hold my aching breath. i walk these same streets as those who will never know me, but i already feel as if i know them better than they will ever know themselves. i turn around sometimes when walking by myself, because i swear i see you, then i start walking in that direction. it never leads me to you, but it does take me to places that have you in them; be it a song, a drink, a smell, a laugh. there is so much of you still lingering with me, i know i will never not be without you. that alone brings me comfort. that alone makes my solitude feel as though i am not completely by myself. it is what brings life to these words, these feelings, to this body. there is still enough of you here to make it feel as though you never left. you are my ghost, but i will endure your lovely haunting.

love will always be what i am living for. regardless if it is felt mutually, given back to me, or understood by the one i am with. there will be that part of me giving a little more on days where i don't feel my best or feel like giving anymore. i have not changed all that much from when i was a kid. i would look at the street corners while walking downtown and think how lonely that person is wearing clothes that barely fit them. i thought i never wanted to end up like that, but we never truly get our say as to how it all goes. we just hope whatever we give and have to offer will keep us from becoming someone we cannot wrap our arms around. i guess what hurts most is the breathing some days. the feeling of not even being enough for yourself. the waking up and realizing you are still alone in a bed made for two. other things hurt me, but knowing i have almost given my entire life to love without having anyone to show for it hurts more times than not. but i am thankful i am still here. i am thankful i am still breathing no matter the pain that cannot escape when my exhales feel like a submission and i cannot get away from. i want to say the hard part is over, that no more heartache will find me, but we all know as long as you are alive, there is a chance it will always find you. it is what makes life what it is, and for most of us, us givers, empaths, introverts, we cling to any energy we feel and try our hardest to resist the enticement of giving in to what it is we feel that is never ours to tackle. there is always someone else who needs us or so we think. it is a sucker punch to the soul, yet we get back up and fight like hell to feel again. sometimes, it is only after the goodbye do we hear the hello. the smells and sensations of love will never leave me. i will forever remember each lover that has crossed paths with me. though each one ended in loss, regret never steps in to take its place. each and every passing comes with something new to offer. a new feeling to sit down with and get to know. maybe the next time she won't leave and love will get an opportunity to share itself with both of us. love is still love even if it chooses to go. it is why i cannot give up. it is why my heart still carries a room for you.

she is mostly scattered across the sky these days, but still has time for herself when love is what she needs, when a breath finds her, when an idea brushes up against her heart, when the night time beckons her to dance.
she accepts everything that moves her willingly with open arms. when the life she has built needs her to relax, she finds it in calm waters and subtleties gathered throughout the day. her soul has dreams older than this earth which keep her grounded. her eyes have held more than just a glance at the moon. there is no single right way to love or to care for someone like her. you just hope that your best can run wild with hers and be there when all the stars collapse and create a moment where everything is where it is supposed to be. when life wakes you up gently to ask if you want to see the sunrise and have a cup of coffee, i hope you have it in your hands.
i hope you walk out together. she isn't your best days.
she is the only fucking day that matters, because without her, there is nothing but demons trampling dreams that you could only pretend to sleep with.
she is someone you can never hold back, because she isn't from the same place you are. love has found her more times than it has broken her heart. she is the reminder to live your life without regret. she is the epitome of sacrifice given to the cause of her soul.
where she goes, the moon follows. you can only hope she has room for you in her life, because she isn't one to wait around until the timing is right.

i wish i could tell you, i love you, but we aren't there yet.
i am still trying to understand my place in my own life.
i am still trying to value the words i say to others that i
need to listen to. but i must tell you, you are the most
beautiful woman i have ever been around. you are the
most beautiful soul under the stars. you are a new kind
of beautiful to me. so forgive me if i am at a loss for words.
most of the time, i write better than i speak. i run away
better than i show up on any given day. i listen better than
telling you what you should or shouldn't do. but i am still
learning how that is not who i want to be anymore. i know
in order to have you, i will have to look at you like no man
has ever before. i will have to hold you like no ocean ever
has before. i am going to have to be the best version of me,
and that will be a tall task for someone who is still learning
this version of himself. you are the amen after an uncommon
prayer. you are the touch of red paint on a canvas of white.
you are the first day of winter all wrapped in sunlight and
snowflakes. the only way for me to have you understand my
thoughts, is to be closer to you. the only way this is going to
work, is if i am beside you. this past year nearly killed me,
but i honestly believe it was preparing me for what it will
take to be with you. i want to wake up where you are.
i want to watch you drink your first cup of coffee in the
morning, while i drink mine and write about you and how
you look in the morning when the light hits you just right.
i do not know who you are completely, but i do know your
heart. your eyes show me its love, and in return, i will forever
show you mine. you are the moon's breath, so forgive me if
i stare too long at you while you breathe. i will do my best
to capture who you are in these words, but you will remain
free throughout it all. someone like you is just wild enough to
keep me insane. it is something i would never want to change.

i have learned how much love is inside of me this year.
i have learned how much of i can give until i am broken in-half,
barely breathing, but still wanting to give more. i have learned
how much of my soul is movable when my body insists on resting.
i have learned how a soulmate doesn't always stay and its definition
is loosely based on what we accept in the end. i have learned how
love and death both feel the same when you are lying on your back,
looking up at what used to keep you from breaking. i have learned
how a face can change with every season it kisses and presses up
against. i have learned how lies hold more truth once you begin
to question who you are with. my hands have typed thousands of
poems over the years. each one specifically meant to make you feel,
think, reflect, and possibly feel love in every place of your life you
had been without it. i have gripped mountains and their edges.
i have carved new sky out of the darkness my eyes kept hid behind.
i have fallen in love every hour with a new song, feeling, doubt,
and pretty face that leapt from magazine covers, pretending to be
someone i could die with one day. i have forgotten how it feels to
be talked to with sincerity, with authenticity. i have replaced my
perceptions with someone else's invention of what a partner is,
what a life partner truly is and could be. the thing is, i do not
fucking know how not to love. it could be the devil and i would
still steal flowers from a garden i walked by, just to see a smile
where a crown used to shine. where the frown speaks more about
who they are rather than a smile full of ache. it fucking makes
me cringe and remember my own. i will always be this way; half-
magician, half-believer in my own magic. i am stronger because
of what you didn't do, because of what you couldn't do, because
of what you never thought i was worthy of. I have heard about
the devils and looked them all in their eyes. when it comes to
fear, mine has gone away. the fire may take the man, but the
soul is never taken alive. nothing in this world stains my blood.
i am no longer a victim. i have become my greatest victory march.
it doesn't hit you until it is over and then you realize how achingly
lovely it was to be missed by someone who gave you their best
days. now, you are walking down the street with empty hands,
hoping your entire body stops hurting. hoping somehow you
can find peace in your own company, when someone else held
you together.

i stare at my hands and wonder why they feel so heavy and empty when i have
my love there. i remember they used to touch you in places no one else could
find but me. i remember how they would hold your darkness during the day.
they were good to you when they had caused me immense pain before i met
you. they were so unforgiving and relentless to destroy anything just to say i
had the power to do such a thing. they seem useless these days unless they
are writing about you or holding the string that ties the moon to the sun
tightly so they are constantly in a connected phase. i wish they could write
you in these words again. i wish they knew the strength behind a covered
face when pressed against my own. i wish they knew how to let go of
something that has already released them back to me. but my hands, soul,
and body, they do not understand the concept of catch and release. i have
climbed trees to see how high the fall would be if they were to let go. even
then, it didn't scare me, because i knew love to be an entity that stayed long
after the descent back to reality where nothing stays forever, regardless of
effort. i wish they could touch your face again. i wish they could make that
spark again like they did when amber and ash met face to face and got to
know where the other came from. i wish they knew red and orange the way
a sunset knows a sunrise and how it is just as beautiful when it screams out
for morning. i wish they could bring you back to me, but love stays gone
once it finds a reason to leave the first time. my hands ache. my body sighs.
my heart lingers on. i wish i knew where you went these days when life
shoots you down and out-duels you at your own game. i wish i could lay
with you once more to tell you how every color of the universe exists within
those eyes of yours that make me feel as though i could love you forever.
quiet kisses. simple excuses. sectioned off car rides, stopping only to get out
and stretch out a crooked thought and unbalanced shoulders. it was a dream
i had about you often. though it turned out to be real life only a year later.
i remember the exact day i stopped trying to love you and put you back into
my life. i remember the exact day i left you in a paragraph and pressed a gun
to its temple and pulled the trigger. i buried you with the rest of the year
that almost killed me first. i just wanted you to say something. i just wanted
to know you fucking cared, but you said all you needed to say by leaving
without a fucking goodbye. my hands sill shake when i think about you.
my hands still remain at my side when a thought of you comes out of my
mind and falls below me. i cannot save you anymore. i will not use my wings
to help yours learn how to fly. the blood has dried in my mouth where i tried
biting my tongue off just to keep it from saying your name. but i will always
love you, even if you will never say mine again. tortured souls only know
love in the end, in what becomes of them after dying is over.

these scars came before you, but you loved them as if they happened while we were together. these wounds are still as fresh as blooms kissing sunny skies in may. all of this came before you. i haven't been the same since i was six years old and writing to escape who i was and where i was. i wrote to literally survive the next year of my life as a child. i believed if i could write the pain out, the sorrow, the madness, all of it out, then maybe i could be someone new. i thought i could write my way out of the wrong around me. what a silly thought to have and even more childish to think that could save me from everyone around my soul who had ran out of love by then. i still believe i can save people from where they are. i still believe i can love those who are as broken as i am. my hands have picked up crosses along the way and i carried them for as long as i could until the sin was too much for the nails in my soul to withstand. each word i have ever said to someone, i meant. it wasn't because i didn't love more than i could. it wasn't because love was never enough. time and space have a funny sense of humor when it comes to giving us what we feel like we have earned. it is so fucking cruel for those and to those who give up everything just for a chance at having something we may never know to exist. in some ways, my war paint never gets removed from my face. it is the warriors way. it is the fighter that breaks his hands and face hoping to kiss something soft and forgiving. it is those who struggle day in and day out, just for a taste of honey from a traveling bee heading in the same direction as we march. i have loved all my life. i have lost more times than i have ever won. my scars are my proudest moments. they are my souvenirs, my keepsakes, an actual remembrance of when and where i found out the one i loved, could never love me back the same as we both thought would be forever. some days i am a roaming tiptoe. other days i am making sure i bring down the sky. i am not a happy medium, a perfect center, but i found it once underneath arizona sunsets. i am unsure of where to go next, but everything that has happened to me since the days of discovery, will remain with me. love is doing whatever it takes to outrun the dark, outlast death, and giving all you have to someone who has never known its name. i will find you again, and when i do, do not be surprised if my eyes tell you everything i needed to tell you the first time when i was too shy to even look at you while you were looking at me.

-xoxo

www.ingramcontent.com/pod-product-compliance
Lightning Source LLC
Chambersburg PA
CBHW021952290426
44108CB00012B/1045